WHOLE GRAINS

Grow, Harvest & Cook Your Own

Sara Pitzer

GARDEN WAY PUBLISHING
Charlotte, Vermont 05445

Printed in the United States
Line illustrations, except as credited, by Charles H. Joslin
Woodcuts reprinted by permission from *1800 Woodcuts by Thomas Bewick and His School* (New York: Dover Publications, Inc., 1962).

Front cover photo courtesy of Stephens-Hutchinson Advertising, Inc.

Library of Congress Cataloging in Publication Data

Pitzer, Sara.
  Whole grains.

  Includes bibliographical references and index.
  1. Grain.   2. Cookery (Cereals)   I. Title.
SB189.P55   641.3'31   81-2836
ISBN 0–88266–251–1 (pbk.)   AACR2

Contents

Rye

Introduction

Although the title doesn't say so, this is a book about improving the quality of our lives. As more and more of us look for food in something close to its natural state, free of unnecessary additives, we progress from simple baking and gardening to experimenting with cooking grains which have not been puffed, flaked, and sugared beyond recognition. Having gone that far we itch to try raising the grain in our own gardens.

This book deals with growing and using nine different grains. Any reasonably curious person will probably want to try eating all nine, but even a fanatic with acres to spare is unlikely to grow them all, at least not all in the same year. And so we have included information not only on how to grow and use each grain, but also on how and where to buy it, because being able to find what we don't produce ourselves is a kind of self-sufficiency too.

The reasons we aspire to such self-sufficiency seem to have a lot to do with how well our projects turn out. Watch anyone who has plunged into a spree of growing, cooking, and preserving for the pleasure of it—for the fun of growing, the superior eating, and the sense of being part of nature's cycle—and you'll be watching a successful project.

Those who plant and reap and store food out of fear, to survive a nuclear holocaust or an economic disaster, for instance, may grow fine grain and bake beautiful bread, but they're missing the best part, the sense of *positive* activity that comes from the whole process. We think the information in this book is complete enough so that you could use it for base survival, if you had to, but we hope that you'll be able to use it as we have developed it—to enjoy.

As anyone who enjoys growing, harvesting, and cooking will tell you, much of these processes is intuitive. Some people just know when to plant the wheat and when to harvest it; some cooks just know when the bread dough "feels right." But as anyone new to these mysteries can attest, a few nitty-gritty directions speed intuition along by light years. We've tried to compile the most specific data available about such relatively uncharted areas as growing grains in your garden, harvesting and storing them, and grinding and cooking them.

Our forefathers had this wisdom. It nearly was lost, but we're not too late to save it. In fact, we have an edge on earlier generations because, romantic as they sound, the good old days were tough. People worked hard and wore out young, caught up in the truly endless chores of keeping themselves fed and sheltered. While technology has brought us problems, it has also made life easier in some fundamental ways. Grinding flour, for instance, takes forever if you have to do it by hand; a small electric flour mill grinds it in a flash. Threshing can be so tedious as to make the grain seem not worth the effort; a bicycle-powered thresher turns the job into child's play—literally. To help you decide which pieces of equipment are appropriate for your partic-

1

ular operation, we have included a chapter on small-scale equipment you can buy, make, or uncover in dark corners of antique barns.

We have been less specific when talking about planting times, about seed varieties, and about when to harvest, often advising you to talk to someone like an extension agent or farm store representative or neighbor farmer. That's because such things depend so much on the climate and soil conditions where you are that only immediate human wisdom can answer your questions accurately. Besides, such talk is part of the fun.

And that brings us back to the purpose of this book. We hope it will answer many of your questions and suggest ways of finding answers we haven't provided. We hope you'll find it a book to use and *enjoy*.

Whole Grains for Everyone

A lot of people wrote this book—gardeners, farmers, cooks, tinkerers, teachers, tasters. People from coast to coast contributed their ideas, shared their experiences, and reported on their experiments. Not every experiment succeeded. Crops were lost in weeds and succumbed to drought; experimental breads baked into bricks; devices to hull grains produced more debris than food. But other crops flourished; recipes got rave reviews; gadgets for threshing worked marvelously. Our experiences have produced a small body of wisdom about what works and what doesn't work, about problems you must solve to be successful with grains, and about the ways our own enthusiasm can do us in. The purpose of this book is to communicate to you what we've learned. It's advice.

Everybody knows it's more fun to give advice than it is to get it, but please take time to consider ours anyway. Having digested, evaluated, and perhaps tried it, you'll be able to build on it and add your own discoveries to it, at which point you can take the whole expanded package to someone else and give them advice.

Growing Grains

When it comes to growing grains, following two simple rules will keep the experience positive:

1. Think through the entire process before you begin.
2. Start small.

Preparing the ground and getting the seed in is only the first step in a long process. Each step requires time and energy and planning. You don't want to spend the summer admiring your amber waves and etcetera only to realize at harvest time that you don't know how you're going to cut the grain fast enough to keep ahead of the birds and the thunderstorms. Before you drop the first seed to the ground, you need to answer these questions:

How much grain do I want to harvest?
How will I control the weeds in my grain?
In case of drought will I water or give up the crop?
How will I harvest the grain? Will I need help? Can I get it?
How will I thresh, winnow, and hull the grain? Is there any use growing oats if I can't get them out of the hulls?
Where can I store my grain to beat bugs, rats, and heat?

Equipment

These considerations about growing lead directly to more questions about equipment. You'll have to figure out what you want to buy and what you don't need. Some items, seed cleaners and hullers for example, are so expensive they probably are not worth the cost for the amount of use they'll get unless you go into a communal arrangement with other growers. Some equipment can be improvised. If you're

3

really not growing enough grain to warrant paying for an antique fanning mill, you can manage the winnowing with an electric fan or even the wind.

The piece of equipment you're most likely to want is a home mill to grind grains into flour. Some books suggest using your blender, but it doesn't work well. You can't make nice fine flour, only a coarse meal with particles of uneven size. At first, buying an inexpensive hand-cranked mill sounds right and romantic — back to nature all the way. But how much flour are you going to be grinding? You'd have to grind all afternoon to get enough flour for six loaves of bread and that's apt to discourage you from baking at all after the first few tries.

Electric Mills

Anyone who doesn't have access to endless volunteer labor and wants to grind more than two cups of flour a week probably should invest in an electric mill. As interest in natural foods and whole grains grows, new models of mills, usually priced between $200 and $300, are becoming available regularly. Each has advantages and disadvantages.

For a while the slow-speed stone mills seemed ideal because the stones were supposed to do a better job than steel blades of spreading the oil from the grain's germ evenly throughout the flour and because the slow-moving stones did not overheat the grain as much as rapidly moving stones or steel blades. But in talking with people who own mills, I've learned that the newer steel-blade mills warm the grain less than the slowest stone ones and if the oil is unevenly distributed in the flour, you can't tell. Moreover, cleaning the stone mills can be a chore, and old flour left on the stones turns rancid and spoils the taste of the next batch of flour you grind. So, while you still may prefer a stone mill, you shouldn't automatically assume it will be the best. And, as another complication, you can buy some mills that are a little cheaper because you assemble them yourself. Fine. How handy are you?

The mill you choose will depend on your budget, the amount of flour you expect to grind, and even on what grains you'll be grinding most often. (Oats, for instance, grind better with steel blades. Stones tend to mash more than grind on softer grains. Steel blades are better, too, for peanuts or soybeans, or any kernel high in oil or moisture content. Stone is preferred by those

SPROUTING GRAINS

Grain	Sprouting Time[1]	Sprouting Length	Yield
Barley	3–5 days	length of seed	double amount of seed
Buckwheat	2–3 days	¼–½ inch	triple amount of seed
Corn	2–3 days	½ inch	double amount of seed
Millet	2–4 days	¼ inch	double amount of seed
Oats[2]	2–4 days	length of seed	double amount of seed
Rice, whole brown	2–4 days	length of seed	double amount of seed
Rye	2–4 days	length of seed	triple amount of seed
Triticale	3–4 days	½ inch	four times amount of seed
Wheat	3–4 days	½ inch	four times amount of seed

1. See instructions for sprouting in chapter on wheat.
2. Don't presoak. Germinate between layers of paper towels. Dampen daily.

WHICH GRAIN TO GROW?

If you're a beginner, and want success, your first grain crop should be corn.

Consider the advantage: if you're already a gardener, you're probably growing corn, and you only have to let a few ears go past their prime to have a grain crop. There's no problem of hulls with corn — just husks, and they're easily stripped away. It's easy, too, to twist dried corn off the ear. And you'll be delighted with the corn and cornmeal recipes in this book, and wonder why you waited so long to try cornmeal.

If you're a bit more ambitious, try wheat (or triticale). It's very easy to grow, and you can harvest, thresh, store, and grind wheat in small amounts with little difficulty.

Like those at Garden Way who have experimented with wheat, you will probably grow fond of having a wheat crop, and want one each year. Ah, the thrill of biting into a piece of whole wheat bread and knowing that it is "your" bread, from planting to oven. And don't forget the many other dishes for which wheat is the base.

Rye is the crop for the faint of heart. It's almost immune to failure. It's hardy, so there's little danger from frosts, and will grow in poor soil. It's a good cover crop for the garden, makes a fine green manure to turn under to replenish the soil, and is easy to harvest, thresh, and grind.

All of the rest of the grains in this book involve one more step, and it can be a difficult one. The grains have hulls that must be removed, or at least minimized.

Millet hulls easily; simply rub a handful of grain between your hands and the thin hulls will rub off.

Barley has a hull that fits firmly into the crease of each grain, and is hard to remove. The commercial method of wearing this down is called "pearling." You can pearl small amounts of your own barley crop by popping it into your blender.

Buckwheat, not a true grain, has a kernel shaped like a beechnut, and covered with a hard, inedible hull. By grinding the buckwheat, then sifting out pieces of the hull, a flour can be produced.

Oats are one of the easiest grains to grow, and the hardest to hull. If you're growing oats for chickens or rabbits or horses, they'll handle the problem by ignoring the hull. If you're growing oats to eat, find a method of hulling before you start. A Garden Way experiment worked with some success. The oats were dried for an hour in a 180° F. oven to crisp the hulls. Then the oats were run through a mill with the stones set so that the hulls were cracked but the oats were not ground.

Rice can be raised at home — if. See chapter on rice for the ifs. Here's a delicious grain that can be used in many ways — all of which most of us would forego if we had to raise our own rice.

Remember that all of these can be purchased, ready for cooking or grinding, at natural-food stores, and some of them in your supermarket. They are generally inexpensive, far less costly than foods that have been processed.

If you buy them at places other than food stores, such as seed stores, make certain they have not been chemically treated in some way to prepare them for planting.

Reaping on an Amish farm.

wanting a fine flour, particularly from wheat or corn. To get an equal fineness in a steel grinder, three, four, or even more passes through the grinder may be necessary.)

Unless you are so remote from civilization that you can't find an outlet for flour mills, you should take the time and trouble to see in operation the mill you intend to buy. The literature may glow with praise for the machine, but if it will grind only a half-cup of grain at a time, don't expect to find that information in the write-up. Nor will promotional material tell you if the mill is hard to clean or noisy to run. Check with people you know who have mills and ask for in-store demonstrations. You wouldn't buy a television set without testing its picture; a flour mill represents a similar investment, so don't trust to luck that it will perform as you want it to. Try it before you buy it.

Check these criteria as you shop for a flour mill:

1. Will it handle in a reasonable amount of time the amount of flour you expect to grind?
2. Does it grind without overheating the grain?
3. Is it easy to clean?
4. Can it be adjusted to grind different grains into varying degrees of coarseness?
5. Is it easy to use?
6. Will replacement parts be available if you need them?
7. Is it manufactured by a reputable company that will honor the warranty?

When grinding grain, avoid the temptation to grind large amounts for future use. Grind what

6

you need for perhaps a week, with the unused portion to be refrigerated in an airtight container. Whole grains can be stored for months without loss of taste or nutrition. This is not true with whole grain flour.

Recipes Using Grains

Not all the grain you eat will be ground into flour. As you scan the recipes in this book, you'll find fewer bread recipes than you might have expected. That's because almost every cookbook has recipes for bread. What seems more useful for people experimenting with grains these days are recipes for other ways of eating whole grains—as breakfast cereal, as main dishes, and as side dishes. Most of the recipes you find here grew from the experiments of people looking for

new ways to include grains in their diets. Recipes are not carved in stone. Try these and change them to accommodate your own experiments. As with growing and grinding, a few simple rules will make cooking grains more successful.

First, remember that whole grain, like any fresh produce from the garden, must be completely clean before you cook it. Nothing will turn off those who eat what you cook faster than biting into a mouthful of grit or chaff or even a little stone. The easiest way to clean any grain (rice always seems to need it most) is by putting it in a large pan and running water over it, tilting the pan to run off the dust and chaff that weren't winnowed away, swirling your fingers through the grain to catch any bits of stone, and finally draining it in a sieve or colander.

The second thing to remember is that while whole grains take longer to cook than highly refined ones, you don't want to cook them into

PLANTING THE GRAINS

| | Per 1,000 Sq. Ft. | | Per Acre | | | | | Lbs. per |
	Plant, lb.	Harvest, lb.	Plant, lb.	Harvest, Bu.	Hull	When to Plant	Soil	Bushel
BARLEY	2–3	25–65	75–100	40	H	Early spring, late fall	Sweet	48
BUCKWHEAT	1	33	36–48	15–20	H	After last frost	Sandy, Fast-draining	48
CORN	1–2 oz. per 100 ft. row	6–8 doz. ears	12	750–1500 doz. ears	N	After last frost	Light, sandy loam	56 shelled
MILLET	1	55	30–35	15–60	H	After last frost	Will grow in poor soil	48
OATS	2	50	80–100	60	H	Early spring, late fall	Will grow in poor soil	32 (varies)
RICE	3–4	60–80	140	65	H	Soil and air must be warm	Area must be flooded	45
RYE	3	40–45	90–120	30	N	Winter: early fall. Spring: early spring	Will grow in poor soil	60
TRITICALE	3–6	35	100–180	20–35	N	Early spring	Well-drained, sandy loam	60
WHEAT	3–6	40	100–180	20–50	N	Winter: early fall. Spring: early spring	Well-drained sandy loam	60

NUTRITION IN GRAIN AND GRAIN PRODUCTS

Food (100 gr., or 3.5 oz.)	Calories (cal.)	Protein (gr.)	Fat (gr.)	Carbohydrate (gr.)	Calcium (mg.)	Iron (mg.)	Vit. A I.U.	Thiamine (mg.)	Riboflavin (mg.)	Niacin (mg.)	Vit. C (mg.)
Barley, pearled	349	8.2	1.0	78.8	16	2.0	0	0.12	0.05	3.1	0
Buckwheat	335	11.7	2.4	72.9	114	3.1	0	0.60	—	4.4	0
Bulgur, hard winter wheat	354	11.2	1.5	75.7	29	3.7	0	0.28	0.14	4.5	0
Corn, field	348	8.9	3.9	72.2	22	2.1	490	0.37	0.12	2.2	0
Cornmeal, 1 cup	435	11	5	90	24	2.9	620	0.46	0.13	2.4	0
Oats (oatmeal or rolled oats)	390	14.2	7.4	68.2	53	4.5	0	0.60	0.14	1	0
Rice, brown	360	7.5	1.9	77.4	32	1.6	0	0.34	0.05	4.7	0
Rice, white milled	363	6.7	0.4	80.4	24	2.9*	0	0.44*	—	3.5*	0
Rye	334	12.1	1.7	73.4	38	3.7	0	0.43	0.22	1.6	0
Wheat, hard red spring	330	14.0	2.2	69.1	36	3.1	0	0.57	0.12	4.3	0
Wheat, hard red winter	330	12.3	1.8	71.7	46	3.4	0	0.52	0.12	4.3	0
Wheat, soft red winter	326	10.2	2	72.1	42	3.5	0	0.43	0.11	—	0

* Enriched white rice   This table is based on information in the USDA *Composition of Foods*, Agriculture Handbook 8.

goo. Most whole grains cook to perfect tenderness in forty-five minutes to an hour, at most.

Salt Sparingly

A word about salt. Every time you turn around someone is warning you not to use so much salt and saying you get all you need for a week from one dill pickle. Here's good news. When you cook with whole grains you can easily use much less salt than you ever have before. In experimenting with recipes over the past twenty years, I've discovered it takes very little salt to make any food taste "salted." Recipes calling for as much as a teaspoonful of salt work perfectly well with only ¼ teaspoonful.

The problem comes when you are using the salt to make the food have any taste at all. I began hatching this notion a long time ago as I watched a dinner companion eating a particularly tasteless piece of roast beef. I'd given up on mine, but he was eating away, stopping every few bites to add a little more salt. The people who make most canned and dehydrated soups do pretty much the same thing; salt usually is the predominant taste and is named high up in the list of ingredients, indicating its presence in proportionately large amounts.

If you think about it, you realize that white flour, polished rice, highly refined grains, and the products made from them don't have much taste except for the seasonings added to them.

When the recipe on a package of white rice calls for a teaspoon of salt to cook a single cup of rice, it's because otherwise the rice hasn't any flavor. But whole grains have their own flavor. You may add a bit of salt so that they taste salted, but you don't have to add it so they'll have taste. In fact, too much salt obscures the good flavors. As you check the recipes in this book, you'll notice the amounts of salt suggested are comparatively small. Even if you're accustomed to more, try it this way first, because—honestly—that's all you'll need.

Secrets of Serving

Having offered advice on how to approach growing grains and on how to cook them, let me indulge in a final suggestion on how to incorporate them into the diets of people who still think oats grow in little O's and corn and wheat grow in squares inside red-checked boxes. Do it the same way you'd approach a big black bear—very carefully. Most of us hate to admit it, but we resist change. Probably this includes even you. A person accustomed to food that's bland to the taste and effortless to chew is not going to gobble up his first slice of sprouted wheat bread shouting, "Goody, goody." More likely, he's going to feed it to the dog and head for the neighbor's in search of a Twinkie. And if, after reading this book, you get all hopped up, run out and buy a pound of each of the nine grains you read about, and serve them all for supper tonight, your neighbor is probably going to get your whole family. (Ask me sometime how I know.)

My own experience and that of others who have added whole grains to their meals suggest that the way to do it is to create as little anxiety as possible. Nobody should feel that he or she *must* like anything. All the familiar old favorites shouldn't be replaced suddenly with strange casseroles and dark breads. And no one, especially children, should fear that if they don't like the wheat soup they'll get no supper at all. Instead, include a whole grain dish along with the food you usually serve, with as little fanfare as possible. If somebody doesn't like it, refrain from commenting. And never scream, "How come nobody in this house ever wants to eat anything but hot dogs and vanilla ice cream?" Don't get preachy about nutrition. But don't give up, either. Continue to include whole grains in each meal, beginning with the more familiar ones like corn and rice. Cornbread made from whole-kernel cornmeal couldn't possibly offend anyone, and brown rice is a gentle introduction to a grain without all its nutrients refined away. Save the less familiar grains such as millet and whole cooked rye for later. When you come up with something you like especially well yourself or something that seems to appeal to others, make it again. The change won't come quickly, but in time the people you cook for will come to enjoy and often prefer whole grains.

Corn

In Europe it's *maize*; South Africans call it *mielie* or *mealie*; early Virginia colonists wrote home about learning to grow *pagatour*. Call it what you will, you can't get away from corn. Even if, by some quirk of nature or orthodonture, you were indifferent to chewing it from fresh steamed ears in summer, never touched cornbread, and had Thanksgiving without corn pudding, you'd get yours. It would take a lot of doing to avoid cornstarch and corn syrup and corn oil. And the person who doesn't go for corn flakes with milk may be the same guy who sips a little corn squeezin's after dinner.

Commercial growers choose from the tremendous number of corn varieties according to their highly specific purposes — cattle feed, starch, oil, etc. On the smaller, garden scale, you can plant one or two varieties that will successfully serve all your intentions.

Agriculture students learn to distinguish between flint corn (hard-kerneled varieties good to grow in cool climates) and dent corn (varieties whose kernels develop a small indentation in the center as they dry). They distinguish also between hybrids or crosses and non-hybrid or open-pollinated varieties, and between white and yellow corn.

Field and Sweet Corn

For the home gardener, the most important distinction is between field corn and sweet corn. As you scan the seed catalogs you will see that sweet corn comes in yellow, white, and mixed kernels, and hybrid or open-pollinated, as does field corn. Sweet corn and field corn look alike to all but the experienced eye. Many farmers who grow field corn for feed plant a few rows of sweet corn near the edges of the fields for feeding themselves. (The varieties won't cross if they don't flower — produce pollen — at the same time.) The farmers know, just by looking at the stalks, which is which, but more than one would-be poacher has picked and shucked an armful of ears and rushed them into the pot, only to be disappointed by biting into the tough, starchy kernels of what turned out to be field corn.

Growing Corn

Unless you're growing corn for animals as well as people, growing sweet corn exclusively is probably your better choice. It grows a little less tall and takes a little less room. You can use it not only for eating fresh, but also for drying and grinding into meal. And of course, sweet corn *is* sweeter, no matter how you use it. (Incidentally, animals have absolutely no objection to eating a little sweet corn.)

Most of the sweet corn varieties offered by the seed companies are hybrids, and every year brings new ones. Generally, hybrids taste better, grow better, and resist disease and pests (except for raccoons) better. The only time a hybrid is a poor choice is when you want to save some of your crop for next year's seeds. No telling what, if anything, you'll get next year if you plant saved-over hybrid seed. Even with an open-pollinated variety, the results are none too sure. It depends on your skill in selecting ears from good plants to save for seed and on being certain your seed corn was isolated from all other varieties that might have pollinated it while it was growing. Even in the early 1800s agricultural experimenters lamented that in looking for pure strains they almost never could find "anything more than a mixture." The cost of several ounces of seed a year seems a small price to pay for the certainty that what you see is what you'll get.

Plant Several Varieties

You probably have your own favorite varieties for eating fresh. To insure having corn available as long as possible, choose some of the varieties that mature early and some later; space planting about ten days apart. Don't depend on the spacing to make too much difference, though, because sometimes if the weather has been cool and dry and then turns warm and wet, early plantings and middle plantings will all be ready about the same time, in spite of the difference in planting times. Select your favorites from varieties recommended in your seed catalog for growing conditions where you live.

If you want to get more serious, you'll try raising corn especially for cornmeal. These varieties were developed for shelling after 100 or more days, and are usually left on the stalk until after several frosts.

If you can find a local grower of any of these — and the grower may call it "flint" corn — try it. Chances are it will be good for your geographic area. You can save the best ears you grow for seeds for the next year's crop, since this is not a hybrid corn.

Johnny's Selected Seeds, Albion, ME 04190, carries several varieties. So does Nichols Garden Nursery, 1190 North Pacific Highway, Albany, OR 97321. This company also offers a white-kerneled corn bred especially for making hominy.

Amount to Plant

To calculate how much seed to buy, follow the directions on the packets, which usually tell you how many feet of row the given amount of seed will plant. If you buy the seed loose, figure about one to two ounces per 100 feet of row or twelve to twenty pounds per acre. How much you should plant depends on what you intend to do with it. Dick Raymond's *Down-to-Earth Vegetable Gardening Know-How* estimates 100 to 200 feet of rows should provide corn for a family of four.

Fertile, Sandy Loam

The soil should be richly fertile, for corn is a heavy feeder, and preferably a light, sandy loam. Even commercial agriculturalists who dose their crops with chemicals agree that large amounts of organic matter incorporated into the soil improve a corn crop. Although corn grows satisfactorily in soils with a pH anywhere from 5.6 to 7.7, the ideal seems to be around 6.5, so if your soil is lower than 5.8 add ground limestone before you plant.

Because corn requires much nitrogen, farmers often rotate it to follow alfalfa, which is high in nitrogen. You can get a similar effect by rotating your corn with peas or beans in the garden.

Fertilizing

A complete fertilizer, containing all the basic elements, will also improve your yield. That doesn't mean it has to be a purchased fertilizer. Every elementary school child has heard the story of colonists learning from Indians to fertilize by burying a fish in each hill of corn. One old account estimated that it took about 1,000 fish to plant an acre of corn, and no corn was planted without fish because fish increased the yield by about three times. If you live near a stream where it is easy to catch fish, try planting a few

hills this way and you'll see why the system was so good.

The one thing teachers delicately skipped mentioning in class was that to keep the fish from being dug up, the colonists had a law that every dog had to be tied by the hind leg after corn was planted and kept that way until the fish had decayed in the soil. Manure will do pretty much the same fertilizing job for you, probably with fewer complications.

When you are working fertilizer and organic matter into the soil, don't do too good a job. Experiments have shown that corn germinates and roots grow better when the seedbed has not been too finely worked. The coarser soil is less likely to crust over after rain and allows more air and moisture to get to the seed.

Plant in Blocks

If you are going to plant, say, 100 feet of corn, plant it in four rows twenty-five feet long rather than in one long row, for more complete pollination. If you are going to hoe by hand or with a push-type cultivator, plant the rows about thirty inches apart, leaving twelve to fifteen inches between plants. To use a garden tractor or rotary tiller for cultivation, space the rows according to the size of your machine.

Planting larger areas is more difficult. Some farmers believe the corn planter they use for field corn damages the more tender grains of sweet corn. More spotty germination is their clue, but it's possible also that their sweet corn seed simply isn't as vigorous as their field corn seed. But using even a small tractor to plant the seed takes a lot of space in a fairly uniform block. If this is impractical, you can plant the seed by hand, in time-honored fashion, or you can use a small push-type seeder.

At least one marriage had a shaky spring day on the homestead, however, when a couple tried to plant an entire acre of corn this way. A longer-married homesteader solved the planting problem by giving each of his five children a ruler and assigning them each a twenty-five foot row for their "very own" with instructions to plant the seeds *exactly* one inch deep and twelve inches apart. Their reward was getting to "walk tightrope" back the length of the row at the end of planting, to tamp the kernels firmly against the soil. Good horticultural practice. And who, these days, has the nerve to comment on any child-rearing techniques?

(Once the corn is planted, it would be nice to have those five children to help with the cultivation necessary to keep weeds down.)

Warm Soil

However you plan to get the seeds into the ground, don't make your first planting before the soil warms up to 50° F. — and 60°–95° F. is the best range for germination. Trying to plant earlier in hopes of getting an earlier crop wastes energy and seed, because corn rots in cold soil, and even if the seed lasts until the ground is warm enough, germination will be spotty.

Once your corn is up and growing, your next job is weed control. If you started with a clean plot, this should take only a little hoeing or tilling, but it should be done, even if the weeds aren't actually threatening to choke out the young corn plants, because research has shown that the weeds take from the soil nutrients and moisture the corn needs. With some crops, lettuce or tomatoes for instance, a few weeds don't seem to matter, as long as they don't actually overpower the crop, but remember that corn, being the greedy feeder it is, resents any intrusion into its territory.

Cultivate Twice

Corn usually has to be cultivated twice. After the second cultivation, many gardeners sow annual rye between the rows for weed control and as a cover crop.

Cultivation should be shallow — not more than one inch deep — to avoid disturbing the roots that grow close to the surface.

There's an alternative to all this cultivation — mulching. It works well with corn. Spoiled hay and straw make good mulches. There are many

others. Plant the corn as usual. Scatter hay lightly over the row of seeds, heavier between the rows. When the corn is up at least six inches, add more hay.

Discourage the Birds

In most areas of the country birds are second only to raccoons as enemies of your corn crop. Birds hit early. To avoid this, run two strings the length of the row, a few inches apart and a few inches above the ground. This should be put in place right after you have planted the corn.

For best results, corn, like other vegetables, should grow steadily from sprouting to maturity. Drought sometimes prevents this. If you live in an area where crops are irrigated routinely, be prepared to do the same with your corn. Water deeply but not more often than necessary. Even when the top half-inch of the soil seems dry, you may find it adequately moist an inch or so deeper, especially if you are using mulch and your soil has good organic content.

In areas where watering is usually not necessary, where "dry farming" is the rule, a short dry spell probably won't hurt your corn, especially if you've conditioned the soil with lots of organic matter. During a dry spell one summer in Pennsylvania, an Amish woman marveled, "You wouldn't think it, but the corn just seems to keep on growing." No question, years of working large amounts of straw and horse manure into her garden had helped. In a really dry summer, you have to decide whether you can and want to water or will just settle for a sparse crop.

Harvesting

If all goes well, about seventy to eighty days after you planted it, your sweet corn should be ready to use. Estimates on days to maturity found in the seed catalogs are just that — estimates. In addition to moisture, heat and soil conditions can speed up or delay your corn's development. Check to see if it's ready to be picked. The silk should be brown and dry. Pull down a strip of the husk. See whether the kernels are filled out and plump. Press one kernel with a thumbnail. A milky fluid should flow out. If it's watery, the corn is not ripe; if there is little moisture, the corn has passed its prime. All of a planting of a hybrid will be exactly right for picking for only five or six days—this is the reason for making several plantings of sweet corn.

So far, we've been talking only about the corn you want to harvest for eating fresh, freezing, canning, or drying. For these uses you simply strip the ears from their stalks, husk them, (ideally right in the field), and proceed with your cooking or preserving.

The corn you want to use for meal will be handled differently. You can do as the farmers do and leave your corn standing where it was planted until the stalk is dead and the kernels have dried and shrunk on the cobs. Commercial growers try to dry to a water content of 12 to 13 percent; you'll know when your corn is dry enough because the kernels will shell easily and as they come off the cob, small flakes from the cob will drop into your hand, or, if you're not careful, into your corn container. When storage space is short, farmers sometimes leave corn on the stalks until well into the winter. Snow and freezing won't harm the corn, but blackbirds, squirrels, and bluejays may steal it. Coons will not be interested in your corn at this time. They like it only the day before you are ready to eat it.

Whenever you decide to pick this corn, simply snap the ears off the stalks and toss the ears into a wagon to husk later. Or you can husk as you go along, which has the advantage of saving a trip back to the garden to return the husks to the soil. Either way, dried husks are sharp and hard on your hands, so gloves are a good idea, even if

Old Sturbridge Village photo by Robert S. Arnold

Harvesting the corn crop.

you're tough. Some seed houses and farm stores sell husking pegs. This instrument fits into the palm of your hand and has a sharp point protruding to cut and open the husk. It will speed the job, but it is a nasty weapon that should be kept from children and used cautiously.

If you grew up reciting John Whitcomb Riley's "when the frost is on the punkin and the fodder's in the shock . . .," you may want to try the old method of cutting the corn stalks and bundling them into shocks tied with baling twine, which are left standing in the fields until you want the corn. Some Amish farmers still use this method. It sounds romantic and looks pretty but beyond that, there's not a lot to be said for it. Cutting the stalks is backbreaking. You use a corn knife—a heavy, sharp knife much like a machete or a cane knife, and you have to bend with each cutting stroke to chop the stalks close to the ground. This strains your back in one of its most vulnerable positions. If that movement doesn't get you, bending again to lift the stalks into bundles probably will.

Storing the Harvest

Regardless of how you dry it in the garden, once your corn has been picked, husked, and brought in, the way you store it will depend on how much you have and how long you'll be keeping it.

For small amounts of corn, the most simple method is to strip back the husks, remove some of them, and braid the rest. This is a decorative method, and the braid can be hung where it will dry and where rodents will not nibble at it.

Some oldtimers insist that weevil infestations

Old Sturbridge Village photo by Robert S. Arnold

Husking corn the old-fashioned way.

Corn stored this way may attract rodents.

in corn come more from the residue of previous years' grain than from the new crop. Thus, if you have stored grain in the same spot before, the first step is to clean the area as thoroughly as possible.

One effective, if not unorthodox, way to store corn still on the ear is to hang it from the rafters or a long pole in large net slings. You'll probably have to make these yourself unless you are lucky enough to find some of the large net bags used for storing onions. The simplest way is to buy strong nylon trellis, which is sold in most garden shops and seed catalogs, and fashion it into bags or slings. Be sure to sew with strong nylon twine and make the slings small enough so that the

weight of the corn doesn't strain them to the breaking point.

You need an airtight container for shelled corn. For small amounts, new lard cans work fine. You'll find lard cans in most hardware and farm stores. If not, hardware stores can order them for you. Larger galvanized metal garbage cans are fine too, except that the larger they get the harder they are to move when full.

Plastic won't work. It cracks in very cold weather and when it has been through many temperature changes. You may not notice the cracks right away, but the bugs will.

Corn, like any grain, keeps better in its whole state, so don't grind it into meal much before you use it. The degermed cornmeal on grocery store shelves lasts almost forever because the process used in refining it takes away the germ, that portion of the grain that supports life and contains oil and flavor nutrients. It lasts forever but who wants it?

Your cornmeal, ground from the whole grain, is highly perishable because the fat in the germ can go rancid. How fast that happens depends on the temperature at which you store the meal.

17

One old report on the "keeping qualities of mealie meal" said one batch stayed good for several months in storage, but another, which had been transported across the equator, was unfit to eat when the trip was over. So, in your freezer, cornmeal will keep for several months in an airtight package; stored in the cupboard at mid-summer 85°, it may not last for two weeks. If you have a home flour mill, the best way to get good flavor and nutrition is to grind small batches at a time, keeping only a few cupsful in storage in the refrigerator for quick use.

Buying Corn

If you can't or don't want to grow corn, you can still enjoy it. When sweet corn is in season, many farmers sell it, fresh from their fields, along the roadside. A few will even let you walk into the rows to pick your own. If you buy corn this way and then drive home with it as fast as the speed laws allow, you can serve corn on the cob infinitely superior to any supermarket product.

If you want to buy enough corn for freezing, canning, or drying, call ahead. Many truck farmers will have the produce picked just before you pick it up if they know for sure you are coming.

It is difficult, but possible, to buy good, fresh, undegermed cornmeal. One source is the neighborhood store that carries a few bags produced by a small, local operation. If you get it early in the season it will be fresh. But don't buy bags that look as though they've been on the shelf from November until the following May, because they probably have. Some natural-food

stores sell whole-cornmeal, too. Talk to the store manager about what the store buys and how fast it's sold. Count it a good sign if you find the cornmeal refrigerated. The best test of quality of the meal is to taste a bit. If it is fresh, it will taste "raw" and definitely corny but not strong; if it is stale, it will taste bitter and sometimes even rancid.

Using Corn

The following recipes are for using corn fresh (or green, as our grandmothers called it), dried, and as meal. Many of them go beyond the standard succotash and creamed corn, so you can find new ways to use more corn in your diet.

Fresh Corn

The Indians knew how to get it fresh. Squaws built fires at the edge of the corn fields, set kettles of water to boil, and then picked the corn, which they husked and tossed into the boiling water at once. As much as 90 percent of the sugar in corn changes to starch in the first few hours after it is picked. The Indians knew it without statistics.

Instructions on how to cook fresh corn on the cob differ surprisingly. Katie, the harried Mama in the play "Finishing Touches," spoke for many a cook when she said, "Nobody ever tells you how long to cook corn. I just leave it in there until I get nervous."

If you start getting nervous after about five minutes, you're doing it right.

Cooks differ on whether it's better to steam the corn in a small amount of water or to boil it in a large kettleful. We don't expect to settle the argument, but do prefer the full pot of water because the corn cooks more quickly and evenly. Either way, *do not* salt the water; salt toughens the kernels.

Here is a method used by some southern cooks to redeem corn that's been too long out of the field; *Boil together two quarts of milk, two quarts of water, and one cup butter. Drop in a dozen ears of corn and cook five to eight minutes.* Anybody who can afford to do that can afford to have a servant whose full-time job is finding and preparing fresh corn!

Roasting Ears

Although roasting corn in its husks over hot coals sounds neat when you read about the Camp Fire Girls doing it, in reality the results are often disappointing, producing ears that are burnt on one side and raw on the other. Done right, it's delicious. The following method works well: Open the husks enough to remove most of the silk from the ears, then pull the husks back up around the ears and soak them in cold water for about an hour before putting them on a grate close to the coals. Roast for about an hour, turning frequently. The water that has accumulated in and under the husks will steam the kernels and cook the corn more evenly.

MOCK OYSTERS

12 ears sweet corn, freshly
 picked
1 or 2 eggs
 Dash salt and pepper
1 cup hot oil for frying

Try this old recipe only if you have very sweet, fresh young corn, preferably white.

Husk the corn and with a sharp knife cut down the center of each row of kernels. Use the back of a table knife to run down the rows and force out the insides of the kernels. The mixture will be quite liquid. Allow it to set in a cool place for about three hours, or until it begins to set up into a custard. Beat the eggs, using two if the corn mixture seems stiff, and add them along with the salt and pepper. Mix everything gently but thoroughly. Drop by tablespoonsful into the fat, which should be hot but not smoking, in a heavy skillet. Brown on both sides, drain on paper towels, and serve at once.

MAKES 4–6 SERVINGS

MOCK OYSTER FRITTERS

12 ears fresh sweet corn
3 eggs, separated
2 tablespoons flour
Dash salt and pepper
2 tablespoons oil plus
2 tablespoons butter for
 frying

Cut the kernels from the cobs and beat together with the egg yolks, flour, and salt and pepper. Beat the egg whites separately until they are stiff but not dry, then fold them gently into the corn mixture. Drop the batter by tablespoonsful into the hot fat and fry first on one side and then the other; drain on paper towels and serve at once.

MAKES 4–6 SERVINGS

CORNY CHILI

1 cup small red beans, dry
1 cup good quality lean ground beef or venison
1 large onion, coarsely chopped
½ green pepper, chopped
2 cups tomato sauce
1 cup bean liquid
1 can tomato soup
1 heaping tablespoon paprika
1 cup corn, fresh or frozen
1 to 3 tablespoons chili powder
Salt and pepper

Assume there are at least 25,000 recipes for chili in the world, and this one is still one of the best. It calls for one commercial ingredient you'd not expect to find mentioned between the covers of a book like this — canned tomato soup. The canned soup contains potato starch, which smooths out the chili and gives it a velvety texture. You could accomplish the same thing by thickening some of your tomato sauce with straight potato starch, but in some communities, potato starch is hard to find. If you're enough of a purist to hate being caught with canned soup, substitute one cup tomato sauce, a quarter cup of water, and three tablespoons of potato starch cooked together for five minutes.

Cook the beans ahead of time. Cover them with four cups cold water, bring to a boil, and allow to boil for one minute. Remove from heat and allow to stand with a lid on the pot for two hours. Return to the heat, add a dash of salt, and simmer until the beans are done, usually about two more hours, depending on how dry the beans are.

Brown the beef or venison in a heavy skillet, using no fat unless absolutely necessary. If you can get venison which has been well han-

Glen Millward photo

dled from hunting through dressing out, it will make a pot of chili unlike anything you've ever tasted. You'll be spoiled for beef forever.

When the meat is nearly browned, stir in the coarsly chopped onion and the chopped green pepper and stir until the pepper and onion begin to soften.

Add the tomato sauce and bean liquid and sneak in the tomato soup when no one is looking. Stir in the paprika. Bring to a simmer, lower heat, and cook, on low, covered, for an hour. Check from time to time to see if you need to add a little more bean liquid. About fifteen minutes before serving, stir in the corn, chili powder, and salt and pepper to taste. Simmer briefly so the flavors can blend before serving. Tastes even better the next day if you're lucky enough to have leftovers.

MAKES 8 SERVINGS

CORN SOUP

12 ears corn
4 cups chicken stock
¼ cup butter
¼ cup flour
¼ cup nonfat dry milk
1 cup milk
1 tablespoon sugar
Salt and pepper

This is best made with freshly picked corn, but it is also a good way to use leftover corn on the cob, too. The better your chicken stock, the better the soup will be.

Cook the corn on the cob until it is barely tender. If using leftover, warm it by dropping the ears into boiling water for about a minute. Cut the corn from the cobs, taking care not to get any slivers of cob in with the corn. Set the corn aside and put the cobs into a kettle with the chicken stock. Bring to a boil and simmer gently for about thirty minutes. Remove the cobs and feed to the cow, chickens, dog, or cat.

In a two-quart saucepan, melt the butter and stir in the flour. Cook and stir over low heat until the flour and butter are well mixed and the roux has taken on a light brown color, then gradually add the hot stock, stirring rapidly with a whisk to keep lumps from forming. If something goes wrong at this point and you get lumps anyway, strain them out before you go on.

Dissolve the nonfat dry milk in the whole milk and add to the thickened stock. Bring almost to a boil, but *do not* let the mixture boil. When it is very hot, add the corn, sugar, and salt and pepper to taste. Serve with fresh chopped parsley or watercress on top.

MAKES 6 SERVINGS

MAIN DISH
EGG-TOMATO-CORN CASSEROLE

4 cups cooked or canned
   tomatoes

1 cup corn, fresh or
   frozen

2 slices stale bread, torn
   into small pieces

1 tablespoon sugar

1 tablespoon butter

Salt and pepper

4 to 6 eggs

This is a Pennsylvania Dutch dish, so simple and so good you automatically think of it for Sunday night supper.

Heat the tomatoes to boiling and pour them into a six-cup casserole. Mix in the corn, bread, and sugar. Dot the top with butter and sprinkle lightly with salt and pepper. Break four to six eggs, depending on how many people you want to feed, onto the top of the tomatoes and bake, uncovered, in a 350° F. oven until the casserole is bubbling and the eggs are set. Serve at once.

MAKES 4–6 SERVINGS

CORN FRITTERS

12 ears corn, cooked
   (or about 2 cups left-
   over corn)

1 cup milk

¼ cup nonfat dry milk

1 tablespoon melted
   butter

½ teaspoon salt

Dash pepper

Flour

2 teaspoons baking
   powder

1 teaspoon sugar

3 eggs

These fritters are baked on a griddle like hot cakes and are a good way to use leftover cooked corn.

If you are using fresh corn, cut down the center of each row with a sharp knife and scrape out the kernels with the back of a table knife. If you are using leftover corn, buzz it briefly in the blender or put it through the coarse setting on a food grinder.

Mix the corn with the milk and nonfat dry milk, stirring until no lumps remain. Stir in the butter, salt and pepper. Sprinkle a tablespoonful of flour over the top and stir it in. Continue adding flour, a tablespoonful at a time, until you have a batter that is thin but will hold up when poured onto a griddle. Mix baking powder, sugar, and beaten eggs, then add to the batter, and mix.

Drop by large spoonful onto a hot, lightly greased griddle. Brown first on one side, then the other.

If you find your batter too thin, stir in a little more flour; if it is too thick, add a few spoonsful of milk.

These fritters are very filling served with molasses or maple syrup.

MAKES 4–6 SERVINGS

How to Dry Corn

Pick fully mature sweet corn. After husking, immerse the ears in boiling water for three minutes. Drain and plunge them into ice water for three minutes. This process is to set the milk in the kernels. It also keeps the corn from fermenting or smelling as it dries.

Cut the corn from the cobs and spread it onto large flat pans or cookie sheets. Place these in an oven at the lowest setting or in a food dehydrator or in a protected spot in the sun. Stir occasionally as the corn dries. In your oven it will be a matter of hours; in your dehydrator follow the times given in the instructions. If you dry the corn outside, a tin roof is the best place to put it. And you have to remember to bring all the trays inside every afternoon before the sun goes down so the evening dew won't remoisten the kernels and leave them thoroughly confused about whether they're supposed to be dry or wet. You'll know the corn is dried when it has become very hard and has turned an orange-brown color. Be careful, if you use your oven, not to let the kernels become overly brown from heat. After the corn is dried and cool, store it in an airtight container in a cool, dry place. It will keep almost indefinitely.

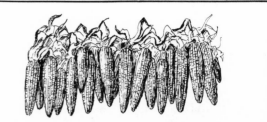

PARCHED CORN

Try something different with your dried corn. Try parching it.

That's what the Indians did with some of their corn, and they taught the settlers to do the same. Many a skin, both red and white, started out on a long trail in those early pre-Revolution days with no more food than a sack of parched corn, trusting in God and a straight arrow or ball of lead to supplement that diet.

To parch corn, place a handful of shelled, dried corn in a greased skillet, and stir it occasionally until done. The moisture in each kernel will make it swell up or even occasionally pop. Don't overcook it; parched corn is a challenge to the molars when cooked to perfection, and if overcooked, can't be eaten.

DRIED CORN AND OYSTERS

1 cup dried corn
4 cups milk
6 eggs
½ cup dry bread crumbs
2 tablespoons melted butter
1 teaspoon whole thyme
¼ cup chopped parsley
½ teaspoon salt
1 pint fresh oysters, drained

Grind the corn in the blender, or pound it with a hammer to break it up. Mix it with the milk, beaten eggs, bread crumbs, butter, thyme, parsley, and salt. Bake, uncovered, at 350° F. for thirty minutes, then stir to mix the corn in the custard, and stir in the drained oysters. Continue baking, uncovered, until the mixture is set, about twenty minutes. Do not overbake or the oysters will become mealy and unpleasant tasting.

Although this recipe is similar to the earlier basic baked corn recipe, you will find it does not turn out as firm because of the extra moisture in the oysters. The bread crumbs absorb some of this moisture.

MAKES 8 SERVINGS

STEWED DRIED CORN

1 **cup dried corn**
Cold water
½ **teaspoon salt**
¼ **cup cream**
2 **tablespoons butter**
2 **tablespoons sugar**
(optional)

Cover the dried corn with enough water to rise about one inch higher than the corn. Place in a cool place and allow to soak overnight. The next day simmer the corn and water gently until the corn is tender and most of the water has evaporated, usually forty minutes to an hour. Just before serving, add the salt, cream, butter, and sugar, and stir. Do not let the mixture boil once you have added the cream.

MAKES 6 SERVINGS

DRIED CORN PUDDING

1 **cup dried corn**
4 **cups milk**
6 **eggs**
2 **tablespoons sugar**
2 **tablespoons melted butter**
½ **teaspoon salt**

This is a traditional Thanksgiving dish in many families. Although this recipe calls for grinding the corn in the blender, you could pound it with a heavy mallet to crush it instead.

Grind the corn in the blender or food processor. Mix it with the milk and beaten eggs. Stir in the sugar, butter, and salt. Pour into a well-greased two-quart baking dish and bake, uncovered, at 350° F. for one hour. About halfway through the baking, stir to mix the corn, which will have settled on the bottom, with the custard.

MAKES 8 SERVINGS

Cornmeal

The number of dishes one can create with cornmeal boggles the mind. If you've been indifferent to it until now, it's probably because you've had only the degermed kind which has a texture like beach sand and not much more taste. When you grind your own cornmeal, or buy it fresh and still containing the germ, you will find it has a fluffy consistency and a sweet-corny taste utterly unlike anything you've tasted before. Your home flour mill will also grind corn. Although you sometimes hear that a blender can also do the job, the resulting meal is coarse and irregular.

To *double* the variety of your cornmeal recipes, try toasting the meal lightly by stirring it over low heat in a heavy skillet or heating it on lowest setting on a cookie sheet in the oven, stirring often, just until it begins to turn color. All recipes taste quite different made with toasted cornmeal. Often, since toasting removes moisture from the meal, you'll find you have to increase the moisture content of your recipes. Just relax and add a little milk or water until you have your usual consistency.

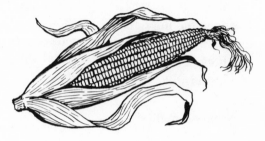

CORNMEAL CORN

When I decided I wanted to grow corn for cornmeal I wrote a man who grinds grain with his water mill for a living. He told me the best corn for cornmeal was a "hard northern flint" corn. At that time (mid-60s) this corn was not readily available. Then I found wide variations in the seed. Over the fifteen years I have grown it I have selected the best ears each year for seed and now have an eight-row cob eight to ten inches long with either (or both) golden or mahogany golden translucent kernels.

This corn is a 120-day variety, and I have had trouble with it crossing with field corn. It does not cross with sweet corn as it flowers much later.

The flavor is delicious — very "corny." Frosts won't hurt the corn. I leave it on the stalk until the bluejays come in the fall and start eating it. Then I pull the ears, strip the husks back, and braid it in three- or four-foot braids that I hang all over the inside of the house.

It stays hanging until February or March when we then take a few evenings to shell it while watching TV. Most of the kernels come off easily if you hold the cob in your hands and twist your hands in opposite directions. Then I store the corn in metal trash cans in a cool place (barn or attic) and probably don't use it until it is a year old. When I run out of cans, I use a muslin sack, which also works fine.

Corn takes a <u>long</u> time to dry and if there is too much moisture it will gum up your grinder, especially a stone grinder. You have to try a little to see when it is ready. I have kept the dry corn five years or more and so far have had no trouble with it.

You <u>can</u> make cornmeal out of any kind of corn. I don't know that the variety is that important. They vary in the amounts of protein and starch, and certainly the flavor, so the kind you use would depend on what you were looking for in food value and flavor — and probably on what is available.

GINNY PEPPER

CORN BREAD

1 cup cornmeal
1 cup whole wheat flour
2 teaspoons baking powder
½ teaspoon baking soda
½ teaspoon salt
¼ cup honey
1 cup buttermilk
1 egg
3 tablespoons melted butter

This recipe is based on one used at the Moosewood Restaurant in New York, whose cooking and recipes have probably done more to spread enthusiasm for whole foods than any other single effort. The difference is that this recipe uses whole wheat flour and cornmeal; theirs uses unbleached white flour. The whole wheat flour produces a darker corn bread. If you'd prefer yours to be pale, substitute an equal amount of unbleached white flour for the whole wheat in the recipe.

Sift together the dry ingredients and beat together the liquids, then stir everything together. Be thorough but do not over-mix or the corn bread will be tough. Spread the batter in a greased eight-inch square pan and bake about twenty minutes in a 425° F. oven.

MAKES 8 GENEROUS SERVINGS

HOE CAKES

¼ to ⅓ cup cornmeal per person
Salt to taste
Enough water to wet the meal to a nice sloppy batter consistency

Hoe cakes won that name because they were (and still are) cooked on a hoe or shovel over an open fire. This is a recipe endorsed by Ginny Pepper, who calls it a "lovely way to eat your cornmeal." She has translated the old recipe to use on your stove.

Mix batter, then drop batter in small cakes into a medium hot, well-buttered frying pan, as you do in making pancakes. Cover and cook about thirty minutes, turning the cakes after fifteen minutes. As the water cooks out of the cornmeal, it steams and cooks it, making a crisp buttery corncake. These are best hot, but still very good when cold.

You can vary the cake you make by varying the amount of water you use in the batter. You can also add flavorings of many kinds—cheese, chopped vegetables, meat, spices, sweetenings, herbs, and many combinations of these.

Hoe cakes, simple to make over an open fire.

CORNMEAL DUMPLINGS

¾ cup unbleached white
   flour
½ cup cornmeal
1½ teaspoons baking
   powder
½ teaspoon salt
½ cup milk
2 tablespoons melted
   butter

These are good with chicken stew.

When the stew with which you intend to serve these dumplings is about done, sift together the dry ingredients and lightly stir in the milk and butter, mixing just until the dry ingredients are moistened. Then drop the batter by spoonsful onto the top of the bubbling stew. Cover and steam (without lifting the lid) over medium heat for fifteen minutes.

When prepared this way, the broth of the stew will take on some of the flour and meal from the dumplings, which will make it cloudy. If you prefer, you can steam the dumplings separately by dropping them into gently simmering water and then transferring them into the stew after cooking them for fifteen minutes.

SPOON BREAD

3 cups milk
1 cup cornmeal
3 eggs
2 tablespoons butter
1 teaspoon salt
3 teaspoons baking
   powder

We think of spoon bread as southern, and southerners traditionally make it with white cornmeal. However, it is even more tasty made with yellow meal. Think of spoon bread as a cornmeal soufflé and you'll have no trouble understanding how to make it.

Mix together two cups of the cold milk and the cornmeal in a saucepan, bring to a low simmer and cook, stirring often, until the milk is absorbed. Cool the mixture slightly. Separate the eggs and beat the yolks together with the remaining milk, melted butter, salt, and baking powder. Beat the egg whites until stiff but not dry. Mix the liquid combination into the milk and cornmeal gradually, stirring with a whisk to avoid lumps. When all is smoothly combined, gently fold in the whipped egg whites and pour the batter into an *ungreased* two-quart casserole. Bake at 350° F. for forty-five minutes. The spoon bread should still be slightly moist when you serve it, so don't overbake and dry it out.

The protein value in this spoon bread is high because of the combination of milk, eggs, and corn. Served with a tomato salad, this could be a complete supper.

MAKES 6 SERVINGS

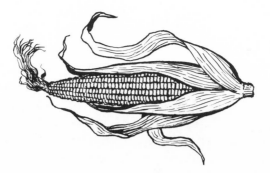

CORNMEAL MUSH

2½ cups water
1 teaspoon salt
1¼ cups cornmeal
1 cup cold water

In South Africa this is called "porridge." If you've been eating corn flakes so long you've forgotten about cornmeal mush for breakfast, try it again now that you're using good meal.

Bring the 2½ cups water and salt to a boil. While you are waiting for the water to boil, mix the cornmeal with the other cup of cold water. As soon as the water is boiling, stir in the cold water–cornmeal mixture, keeping the heat on medium high and stirring constantly to prevent lumps. A whisk helps. Continue to cook and stir until the mush has reached a thick, scoop-out-of-the-bowl consistency. Remove from heat and allow to stand covered for about five minutes. Serve hot with cold milk or cream and perhaps a little brown sugar.

MAKES 6 SERVINGS

FRIED MUSH

Some grocery stores sell mush to fry for almost a dollar a loaf—incredible when you know how cheap and easy it is to make at home. Prepare mush according to the recipe above, or use what is left over from breakfast, and pour it into a greased loaf pan. Chill overnight in the refrigerator. To fry, cut slices about ½ inch thick. Melt a small amount of butter or bacon fat on a griddle, heat to medium, and fry until the slices are crisp on both sides.

POLENTA

5 cups water
1 teaspoon salt
1 cup coarse cornmeal

You could call polenta "Italian mush." The recipe looks much like that for mush, except that you use more water in proportion to the amount of cornmeal and you cook polenta for up to an hour, rather than the short time it takes for mush. The resulting product is fine and creamy, quite different from ordinary mush.

Bring the water to a rolling boil and add the salt. Now begin stirring the water with a whisk, while with your other hand you gradually sprinkle in the cornmeal. As soon as all the meal is sprinkled in, lower the heat and keep stirring. When you have the heat adjusted so that the polenta is simmering gently, switch to a wooden spoon for stirring. Plan other chores close to the stove so you can reach over to stir the polenta often. Ideally, you'd stir constantly, but who tries recipes instructing you to stir *anything* constantly for an hour? So stir often, for about an hour, or until the polenta is very thick.

Glen Millward photo

The Italians traditionally pour polenta onto a large wood slab, make indentations with a big spoon, and pour sauce over the indentations. Then all gather around the table and eat from the common board. If this is a bit folksy for your taste, pour the polenta into a greased pie dish, pour some sauce over top, and cut wedges for everyone, to be topped with cheese and more sauce from a side dish.

MAKES 6 SERVINGS

POLENTA SAUCES AND TOPPINGS

Olive oil
2 cups diced onions
3 cups tomato puree
⅛ teaspoon thyme
⅛ teaspoon sage
½ cup chopped and broiled mushrooms
½ teaspoon salt
¼ teaspoon pepper
2 cloves garlic, crushed
3 tablespoons minced parsley
1 cup grated Parmesan cheese

There's just no end to what you can put on top of polenta. Try a fresh, lightly cooked tomato-onion sauce made with fresh plum tomatoes from your garden and a light sprinkling of freshly grated cheese.

A completely different approach is to sauté a variety of fresh vegetables in a little oil and serve them over polenta. A mixture of zucchini, green onion, green pepper, and chunks of fresh tomato complements the corn taste beautifully.

Or melt some cheese on top of the polenta and use no other sauces.

An Italian friend suggests the following sauce as one that is wonderful with polenta, and can be cooked even while you are stirring the latter. (And you might want to make a double recipe of the polenta to go with this much sauce.)

Pour ⅛-inch layer of olive oil in frying pan, and heat. Sauté onions until golden. Add tomato puree, thyme, sage, mushrooms, salt and pepper, and simmer for thirty minutes, stirring occasionally. Add garlic and simmer for five more minutes. Add parsley and stir.

The serving can be varied by placing polenta on platter, and covering with sauce, then sprinkling with cheese, or by making two layers of polenta, each topped with sauce and cheese.

MAKES 6 SERVINGS

Leftover polenta can be fried like mush and served with syrup or homemade jam for breakfast. This is so good it's worth making extra polenta at dinner, especially if you just happen to have a jar of homemade strawberry preserves.

JOHNNYCAKES I

¾ cup unbleached white flour
¾ cup fine cornmeal
¼ teaspoon salt
1½ teaspoons baking powder
2 eggs, beaten
1¼ cup milk
2 tablespoons melted butter

These are really only pancakes with a little cornmeal added — a good way to introduce the skeptical to cornmeal.

Sift together the dry ingredients; combine the liquids. Stir the liquids into the dry ingredients quickly, mixing only until blended. Don't worry about lumps. Bake on a lightly greased hot griddle and serve at once. You can make these as thick or as thin as you like. Allow the batter to stand for a few minutes to make a thicker johnnycake; thin it out with more milk for a thinner cake.

MAKES 4 SERVINGS

JOHNNYCAKES II

1½ cups cornmeal
1 teaspoon baking powder
½ teaspoon salt
1 teaspoon soda
⅓ cup whole wheat flour
2 tablespoons maple syrup
2 tablespoons melted butter
2 eggs
2 cups milk

These are delicious — *real* johnnycakes, tested on a kitchen full of kids and received with rave reviews.

Sift together the dry ingredients; mix the syrup, butter, beaten eggs, and milk. Stir into the dry ingredients. Mix well, but don't beat hard.

Pour ¼ cup batter at a time onto a medium hot, lightly greased griddle and bake until the edges begin to dry and bubbles appear on the tops, then turn to bake other side. Watch these carefully as the maple syrup in them burns easily.

MAKES 6 SERVINGS

INDIAN CAKES

Use the recipe for Johnnycakes II and substitute three tablespoons dark molasses for the maple syrup. These have a robust flavor that is nice on cold winter days.

MAKES 6 SERVINGS

Erik Borg photo

Popcorn

"Surely," said the male Pitzer, "surely you're going to include a paragraph or two about popcorn."

Surely.

If you choose to grow your own popcorn, handle it as you would any other corn, but remember that some varieties take nearly four months to mature—hard to manage if you have a short growing season. When the kernels are hard and dry, pick the ears, strip back the husks without tearing them off, tie or braid the corn into bunches of about six, and hang in a cool, dry place for several weeks. Then shell the corn and store it in airtight containers, again in a cool place, or better yet, in your freezer.

Some people store their popcorn on the ear until they're ready to use it, but it almost inevitably gets too dry this way and doesn't pop well, since the expanding moisture is what makes the corn pop. Old-time recipes often say "wet your popcorn" as the first step before popping it. If your corn isn't popping into full, tender puffs, try spreading it on a wet towel, rolling up the towel, and letting it stand for several hours.

Considering the space it takes to grow popcorn and the fuss of drying it properly, you may decide to buy yours. It's inexpensive and is one of the few grains to reach the commercial market unadulterated by additives that are supposed to "improve" it. It's sold in all kinds of stores in great variety: white, yellow, hulless, extra large, gourmet hybrid, and so on. The most

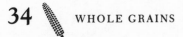
costly isn't necessarily the best. Just keep trying until you find the one you prefer.

To pop popcorn, a deep iron dutch oven with a lid works well. A half-cup popcorn pops up into about four cups, and you'll get the best results if you merely skim the bottom of your pan with oil, then allow it to heat *almost* to smoking before putting in a layer of popcorn only about one kernel deep. It's better to make two batches than to overcrowd the pan. Shake the pan over high heat, occasionally tilting the lid to let steam out.

Try popcorn without the butter for a low-calorie snack. You'll soon prefer it that way.

And for the times when you crave a touch of sweet, here's an easy carmel corn recipe.

CARMEL CORN

1 cup molasses or corn
   syrup
2 cups sugar
1 tablespoon butter
2 tablespoons vinegar
½ teaspoon baking soda

Boil the molasses, sugar, butter, and vinegar together, stirring until a small amount dropped into cold water will crack. Remove from heat, add the soda, and beat vigorously. Pour the candy over a large bowlful of freshly popped corn. Mix.

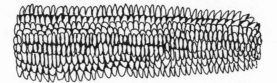

EVEN SIMPLER CANDY CORN

1 tablespoon butter
¾ cup sugar
3 tablespoons water

Mix all together in a saucepan and boil, without stirring, until the mixture begins to make threads when you lift the spoon. Pour at once over about four cups of popped corn and stir until all the grains are coated. Don't let anyone taste until the hot sugar has cooled or you'll end up treating second-degree burns of the mouth instead of sitting around eating popcorn.

Wheat and Triticale

If you're deep into gardening and self-sufficiency, sooner or later you'll want to try growing your own wheat, if only to get yourself away from the process that grows a perfectly good grain, scrapes off the bran, peels out the germ, bleaches the flour, and then sells all those things back to you separately, in plastic packets.

When you try, you'll discover wheat is easy to grow almost anywhere in the United States, even as a wide-row crop in your garden. And you'll feel deep satisfaction in seeing your own grain waving in the breeze. (This to the music of *America*, with its "amber waves of grain.")

But stop the music. Practicality shoulders in. Your wheat is ripe; it must be cut, gathered, threshed, cleaned, and stored. And suddenly everything works against you. If you leave the grain in the field too long, it may shatter and fall to the ground. The birds wait to move in to help harvest, and a hungry band of mice awaits the opportunity to challenge your storage system. And so, trying to beat the birds, you run to your homesteading book and look under "grain threshing," trying to figure out how to get the stuff out of the fields and into the flour bin. You'll find something like this: "Ask a neighbor who has a combine to thresh it for you." Sure. Even if you have a combine-equipped neighbor within thirty miles, he probably would hesitate to put that splendid mass of machinery into motion to harvest a small crop — assuming he could even maneuver it into your garden.

But there are ways to harvest wheat, and other grains too, on a small scale. The simplest ways take a lot of muscle power; a quicker one requires a bit of brain power and makes threshing easy. Before you can harvest, though, you've got to raise the wheat.

Growing Wheat

Select a weed-free area. You can grow the wheat in a solid block, a sort of mini-field, or you can grow it in wide rows. One homesteader plants in four-foot wide rows that allow him to reach in from both sides to pull out weeds as they came up. For an even smaller amount, you can plant a band of wheat at one end of your garden, making sure it doesn't shade any vegetables that need full sun.

A sandy loam with a good balance of nutrients and a pH of about 6.5 is ideal. You don't want a high-nitrogen soil because it will make the stalks grow too fast and tall without improving the actual grain, and such stalks tend to topple over (lodge), making harvest difficult and dropping grain onto the ground.

Wheat needs phosphate. On a small plot you can use bone meal at the rate of about twenty pounds per 1/8 acre, thrown on *before* tilling. Rock phosphate works well too. Till and work in the fertilizers as you would prepare the seedbed for any other garden crop. The size area you plant and the variety of wheat you choose to grow depend on how much you want and what you plan to use it for as well as on the climate in your area.

Here are some figures from Ginny Pepper of Garden Way for 1979. On 5,223 square feet (about ⅛ of an acre) of garden in Vermont she planted thirty pounds of winter wheat and in July harvested 250 pounds of grain in fifteen hours. Broken down that means that on 1,000 square feet (think of a space twenty feet wide by fifty feet long) she would plant about six pounds and could expect to harvest nearly fifty pounds. Harvesting would take about three hours.

A very old agricultural text says a pound of wheat will ultimately produce about a pound of bread.

A word of caution before you enthusiastically

plan to put in enough wheat on your first try to make all the bread you expect to need for the next year. Consider a small trial area the first year so that you can learn how the grain behaves, what its cultivation problems are, how long it takes you to handle it, how it is affected by varying climate conditions, and so on. This way you can avoid the experience of the Pennsylvania homesteader who planted an entire acre in wheat, by hand, only to find she couldn't keep ahead of the weeds, and, when drought struck, couldn't afford to irrigate. Her wheat died and she's now resigned to buying it for grinding in her home flour mill. Ultimately she'd have had more yield and less grief from a modest, manageable row in her garden.

Once you've decided how much to plant and your ground is prepared, you'll have to decide what type to plant. It's easy to get confused about types of wheat. *Winter wheats* are planted in the fall and harvested from June in the South to late July in the North. They're fine for bread and cookies. *Spring wheats* are planted in the spring, harvested in the fall. They yield less than winter wheat. Most have a high gluten content, so are good for breads. Both spring and winter wheat are further divided into *soft wheats*, lacking a high gluten content and used primarily for pastries and crackers; *hard wheat*, with a high gluten content, used for bread; and *durum wheat*, only a spring crop and used for various spaghetti products. (See table.)

The variety you select depends on where you live. Check with an Extension agent, local farmers, or your seed store to find the right varieties for your area from among the 300 or so available nationally. Some homesteaders say winter wheat is ideal for making bread, and where it can survive the cold, it has the additional advantages of being ready to harvest before the mad rush of fall when everything in the garden seems to be ready at once. Also, in areas that are wet in spring, it's hard to start a spring wheat crop early enough.

There isn't a great deal of difference in the cost of seed wheat from a seed store and the wheat you can buy in a health-food store. The advantage of getting it in a natural-food store is that you'll probably have a wider choice and you can try eating some before you buy it to plant. If you find a variety you particularly like, you can save part of each year's harvest for planting the

COMMERCIAL CLASSES OF WHEAT

CLASS	Hard Red Spring	Durum	Red Durum	Hard Red Winter	Soft Red Winter	White
WHERE GROWN	North Central States	North Central States esp. N. Dakota	North Central States	Southern Half of Great Plains	Eastern States	Far West
USE	Bread	Pastas	Pastas	Bread	Pastry, Biscuit, Crackers	Pastry, Puffed and Shredded Breakfast Foods

Wheat harvest on Amish farm.

following year. The possible disadvantage is that the wheat carried in your natural-food store may not be ideal for growing in your particular area.

Plant winter wheat to allow for six to eight weeks of growth before the soil freezes. This allows time for good root growth. If the wheat is planted too early it may smother itself the following spring and could be vulnerable to some late summer insects which would be stopped by cool weather a little later. If winter wheat is planted too late, the roots may not develop enough to stand the cold, and the wheat will not winter well. This may depend somewhat on the quality of your soil; some researchers believe excessively wet land that puddles and freezes chokes the plant when it freezes over, depriving it of oxygen. At least theoretically then, dryer land would support wheat at lower temperatures.

Spring wheat should be planted as early as the ground can be worked. Do the initial plowing in the fall and then till and sow in the spring.

To insure a fairly evenly distributed crop, figure out the amount of seed you'll need, divide it into two piles, and broadcast one part in one direction, such as east and west, and the remainder in another, such as north and south. A cyclone crank seeder will do an even job, but for a small plot, broadcasting by hand is fine, and for planting in rows is probably the best approach.

Cover the seed by rototilling or raking it in to a depth of 1 to 1½ inches for spring wheat, 2 to 2½ inches for winter wheat. Then roll it with a lawn roller, or, on a small area, put down a plank and walk on it, to firm the bed and increase the contact between the seed and the soil.

With a fall planting and cooperative weather, the wheat should be five or six inches tall by winter. The following spring, as early as you can get on the land without wallowing in mud, roll the wheat again. This is an old practice that increases the number of stems emerging from one crown by squashing the crown and stimulating the plant to grow more stalks. The process is called tillering. After this, just keep the weeds down, if you can, and enjoy watching your wheat grow until harvest time.

As you admire your rows of wheat, you'll notice in midsummer (later for spring wheat) a change in them. The color of the stalks turns from green to anything from yellow to brown. The heads, heavy with grain, tip toward the earth. It's time to test the grain. Pick a head, pick out a few grains, and pop them into your mouth. If they are soft and doughy, the grain is not yet ready. Keep testing daily. One day the grains will be firm and crunchy. It's time to harvest.

Harvesting

At harvest, how should you cut it? If you have a very small plot, you won't. Instead, you'll just pick the heads of wheat off the stems. It goes quickly if your wheat field is no larger than about six feet wide by twenty-five feet long.

If you like the old-time way of doing things and are going to harvest a larger amount of grain, you might try to find or build a scythe and cradle; or see listing in Appendix for one firm manufacturing a cradle. The scythe itself is not unusual. What is different is the cradle, a series of long wooden fingers mounted above the

Homemade rack attached to tractor.

Cutter bar drops grain on it.

Driver can dump filled rack.

scythe blade. The scythe cuts the wheat, then the cradle carries it to the end of each swing, and deposits it in a neat pile, stacked so that all of the heads are grouped together in each pile. You can cut with the scythe alone — these are easy to find — but you'll waste a lot of time picking up the cut wheat and arranging it so it can be handled easily.

Another possible tool for cutting small amounts of grain is the sickle. It's a matter of grab and cut, grab and cut. If you're right-handed you'll hold a handful in your left hand and swing the sickle with the right to cut at near ground level. It's possible to kneel or crouch in various postures to avoid getting too tired. As you cut handfuls, lay them in small piles with all heads pointed in the same direction.

The next step is to bind the grain into sheaves, each about twelve to fourteen inches in circumference — a bunch you can hold comfortably in your two hands. Bind the same day you cut the wheat. It's nice to have two people taking turns cutting and sheaving. You can bind with cord or baler's twine or even with some of the wheat

To use grain stems to tie sheaves . . .

Using a sickle is easy way to cut small amounts of wheat. Crouching eases back strain.

Make a simple knot with stems.

"Hats" on stooks discourage birds.

Press knot against sheave, circle sheave with stems, and tie. It takes practice.

A stook is a group of sheaves.

stems, twisting them in a way that holds the bundle firm. From eight to twelve sheaves are piled together to form a shock (also called a shook or a stook). To make a shock or shook or stook, push the bases of two sheaves firmly in the ground at about a 60° angle, leaning toward each other, then mesh the tops of the two sheaves for stability. Mesh two more and place them at right angles to the first pair, forming a square. Pile as many as eight or ten more around them. A cheesecloth "hat" on top of the stook discourages hungry birds. The stooks are left in the field for a week or ten days, curing, even during wet spells. Rain doesn't harm the grain.

Threshing

Then it's time to thresh the grain, to separate the straw and chaff from it. You can go about it in any number of ways.

One method is *flailing*. A *flail* consists of one piece of wood about three feet long, which is the handle, attached with a leather thong to a shorter piece about two feet long. The shorter piece is flung at the grain repeatedly, shattering a few heads each time. When Ginny Pepper tried this method she produced about three pounds of wheat in twenty or twenty-five minutes. That's slow work. Also, there's a trick to learning to swing the flail without rapping yourself on the head.

Another Garden Way experiment was to try beating the individual sheaves inside a large, clean trash can. In two hours the threshers produced a can full of wheat, but with a lot of chaff and even solid heads in it. This was faster than flailing, but produced far more debris that had to be separated from the wheat.

Next they tried beating the sheaves by swinging them against a piece of plywood on which were mounted two cross-pieces of wood, with the plywood leaning against a wall. This worked somewhat better than the other two methods, producing one and one-half cans of very chaffy wheat in two hours.

All these methods turned out to be slow, hard work for the amount of grain produced. The threshers wished they could find and use one of the old stationary threshers popular in the days before combines. They'd heard of a Japanese thresher which would do the job, but the cost of more than $1,000 didn't seem like a good idea for the relatively small amount of grain in question.

Then one evening as Ginny was watching a television program about Asia, she saw a brief scene of people threshing rice. They were using a large drum that spun away from them, and apparently the drum had nails sticking up from its surface. She described it to Kim Bronson of Garden Way, who was helping with the wheat. Kim made a drum, using a utility wire spool and devised a method of spinning the drum by using a pedal, a bicycle chain, and some other parts of the bicycle.

The next attempt used more of the bicycle, so that one person could sit on it and turn the drum, while another person fed the sheaves heads-first onto the drum so that the nails would pluck off the grain. With this they threshed out 250 pounds of wheat in 5¾ hours, and found the

Spool with nails threshes wheat.

Bar at left is linked by bicycle chain to spool . . .

So that spool rotates when bar is pressed.

One person can operate thresher.

work much easier than any of the methods involving beating. They found, too, that they could do much of the preliminary winnowing simply by lifting a quantity of the grain in the lid of one of the storage trash cans and pouring the grain back into the thresher box, letting the wind carry away the chaff.

Winnowing

The usual method for winnowing is pouring the grain from one container to another, letting either the wind or the breeze from an electric fan push the lighter chaff out of the grain, but it's nearly impossible to get the grain perfectly clean with this method and you end up picking out a lot of debris by hand. Sears sells a $230 seed

Alternate method is to hook bicycle to thresher for power.

Seed cleaner winnows wheat.

cleaner that is powered by electricity. This is expensive but would be practical for a group to purchase and share.

And on a very small scale, one determined woman devised a way to clean a few cupsful of grain at a time, for cereal, using the high speed on an electric hair dryer.

Storing

The way you store grain depends on how much you're dealing with. Storing it properly means protecting it from heat, light, and moisture, as well as rats, mice, and insects. You can keep a small amount of grain in plastic bags in your freezer practically forever; it takes more effort to store larger amounts.

Mormons are good teachers about storage because they emphasize being prepared for emergencies by having enough food stored to last a

year. One of the basic foods they store is wheat. Thus they know well the problems of storing grains and have worked out methods to insure that the grain will be in excellent condition for at least a year.

Mormon authors recommend storing hard winter or spring wheat with less than a 10 percent moisture content, a moisture level that is difficult to attain without artificial drying.

Five-gallon metal cans with paint-can friction lids are ideal for storing all grains. One hundred pounds of grain can be stored in three of these. New lard cans, which hardware stores can order for you if they don't already have them in stock, also work well. Garbage cans are not good for storage because it is difficult to make them airtight.

While these cans will prevent new insects from getting into the grain, you must take another step to eliminate any eggs or larvae already in the grain. A simple method is to heat the grain in your oven for thirty minutes at 140° F., which also will help reduce the moisture content. If you're not sure about the accuracy of your oven's thermostat, check it against an oven thermometer, because temperatures higher than 140° may damage the grain.

For a greater amount of grain, you can use dry ice—carbon dioxide. Wear gloves when handling the dry ice. Place a shallow layer of grain in the bottom of the can, add about two ounces of dry ice (figure on a half-pound of dry ice per 100 pounds of grain), then fill the can with grain. Place the lid on top of the can, but don't press it into position. You want to let the vapors of the dry ice force out the oxygen. If the can lid is on firmly, the lid could be blown off or the can could explode. After a half-hour, place the lid on firmly, but watch the can for another half-hour for any signs of bulging. If this does happen, gently lift off the lid, then replace it. The initial fumes will kill any larvae and insects, but those fumes must be contained in the can if the eggs are to be prevented from hatching. For this reason the can must be airtight. If you have doubts about the can, seal it using insulating tape or wax.

If you are reluctant to handle dry ice, you might try this method used in earlier times in South Africa for storing corn. Fill the airtight can nearly to the top with grain, place a lighted candle inside and cover the can. When the candle has burned up all the available oxygen, the flame will go out and, in the absence of oxygen, insects will not thrive. Reports differ on whether this method kills weevils present or keeps new ones from appearing or both, but if you live where winters are very cold and you will be storing your cans in a cold place, the candle approach should be adequate.

Another fumigating method is to drop a piece of calcium carbide into a tin can of water, place the tin can inside the storage can on top of the grain and cover the grain container. The carbide will bubble in the water, producing acetylene gas. As with the dry ice, you would first leave the lid on loosely, tightening it later and watching for signs of bulging. This is probably the least effective and most dangerous method you could use.

Whichever method you choose, keep the cans off a concrete floor, to avoid rusting. Place them on shelves, or on a board on the floor.

Grant Heilman Photography

Triticale

Almost everything you've just read about wheat is true also of triticale (pronounced tre-ti-cay'-lee). The grain is a cross between wheat and rye, developed in the 1960s, although agronomists had been trying much longer to make a good rye-wheat hybrid. Triticale is not a hybrid in the sense that if you plant grain from your crop it will not revert to parent types in subsequent crops. This is because the grain was produced with some man-made chemical and mechanical interference, removing the embryo from a crossed seed that would not grow and growing it artificially in a culture, and before that, treating plants with an alkaloid called *colchicine* to change their chromosome structure. That's a lot of activity beyond the simple pollination of one plant from another.

The object of all this experimentation has been to produce a kind of "super grain" with the yield of wheat, the winter hardiness of rye, and a protein value better than either. So far, the resulting grain has not lived up to its billing, although it *is* a valuable addition to the grains we can cultivate. Back in 1963 Warren Leonard and John Martin reported in their classic agricultural text, *Cereal Crops*, that so far heat treatment and colchicine treatment of the rye-wheat crosses had not been of practical value. It wasn't until 1967 in the research at the University of Manitoba in Canada and at the International Maize and Wheat Improvement Center in Mexico that results began to be promising.

The triticale available today is higher in lysine than wheat, has good protein value, and tastes a little stronger than wheat but a little milder than rye. So far it has not always yielded as well as wheat and it still is not as hardy as rye. However, on the garden level neither of these factors is too significant, since you are not trying for a commercially impressive yield. If you decide to try growing triticale, plant, cultivate, harvest, and store it exactly as you would wheat, allowing for the fact that some people still report that

it is not as hardy as winter wheat in severe climates. If you have trouble finding seed, you can buy some at a natural-food store or order it from a seed company. When it comes to using triticale you will find it can be treated just about the same as wheat too.

Buying Wheat and Triticale

Although it's hard to predict where you will find triticale and in how many forms, you can buy wheat almost anywhere food is sold, except for McDonald's perhaps, and in a tremendous number of forms. Let's assume everyone is familiar with the supermarket offerings of bleached and unbleached white flour, whole wheat flour, and, occasionally, graham flour. You've probably used some or all of these flours from time to time, knowing as you did so that they weren't very valuable nutritionally if they were bleached and enriched, and that if they were whole wheat they were losing quality in nutrients and taste every day they stood on the shelf. Realistically, unless you are a committed purist, you'll probably never give up those products entirely. For one thing, sometimes the effort it takes to keep yourself supplied with home-produced wheat flours to the exclusion of all else is more than you can manage; for another, not everyone has easy access to a good natural-food store.

Just to get some perspective on the issue, let's look at all the wheat products offered and try to consider their respective values. We won't be talking about prepared wheat products such as wheat crackers or *Wheaties* or store bread—only about the basic wheat-as-ingredient products.

Berries. The whole wheat grains are called berries. They have not been cooked, mashed, or otherwise changed. If they are in good condition, they will sprout and can even be used as

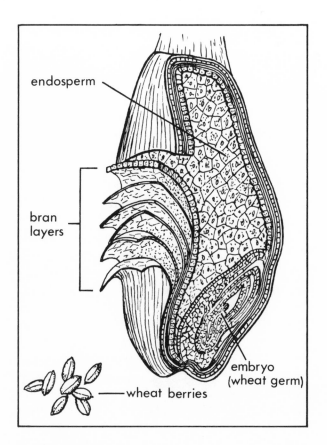

endosperm

bran layers

embryo (wheat germ)

wheat berries

seed. You can buy wheat berries in natural-food stores, from feed stores, and from farmers who grow wheat for their livestock or for commercial flour manufacturers, and sometimes from small local flour mills.

If you buy wheat berries anywhere but in a food store, be very certain they have not been treated with any chemicals or fungicides that make them unfit for human consumption.

Wheat berries can be cooked a long time to make porridge and they can be cooked with less liquid for a shorter time to use much as you might use rice. With a blender you can grind wheat berries into a coarse meal; with a home flour mill you can grind your own wheat flour. Berries you buy in a natural-food store should be clean and stored in a cool dry place. Grain you buy from a farmer will probably have to be cleaned to remove residual dirt and chaff which don't bother animals but would upset most people.

Bran. The outer coating of the grain, which is scraped off in refining processes, is the bran. You can buy straight bran, bran flakes, and another processed bran cereal which looks a lot like tiny worms, usually sold as "whole bran." Straight bran is usually easiest to find in a natural-food store; the other two cereals are common on grocery store shelves. If refiners didn't take it off the grain in the first place, you wouldn't have to buy it at all. Bran's main value is as bulk or roughage in the diet. Bran muffins are famous, but you can add bran to a diet in more subtle ways by mixing small amounts into such foods as bread, cereals, and quick breads.

Bulgur. Or *burghul*, or *bulghar*, depending on who's spelling it, is wheat berries which have been steamed, parched, and cracked. You can buy it ground coarsely or finely, in bulk in most natural-food stores, and boxed in a surprising number of grocery stores. You can also make it by boiling the wheat berries about half an hour, until they are barely tender, draining them thoroughly and toasting them in flat pans for about an hour in a warm oven until they are completely dry. Finish the process by grinding the parched berries to the degree of fineness that suits your taste.

Cracked wheat. This is the whole berry, uncooked or processed, that has been cut with steel blades into coarse pieces. It cooks faster than whole berries but not as quickly as bulgur. Natural-food stores and some grocery stores sell it. If they don't have it and you ask, they can order it for you.

Flours. We'll disregard the grocery store offerings of bromated, bleached, pre-sifted, and instant flours as products resembling ground styrofoam more than food. *Unbleached white* flour also has been refined but has not been treated further to make it whiter. It is available now from all the major flour manufacturers in most supermarkets. This is always enriched. However, in natural-food stores you sometimes find unbleached, *un*enriched white flour, and one company sells an unbleached white flour which has had some of the wheat germ returned to it. (You can do the same thing yourself for less money.) And as if that weren't enough confusion, unbleached white flours are now sold marked "all-purpose," "pastry," and "strong bread." When you can find it, the best buy among these is the strong bread, because it is higher in protein. You can use it for pastry by sifting together two or three tablespoons of cornstarch with each cup of flour. This dilutes the gluten. The best use for unbleached white flour is in combination with whole grain flours when you want to bake a lighter product or when you are introducing whole grains to someone who is used to eating white-flour goods exclusively. Think of unbleached white as a compromise flour.

Whole wheat flour used to be called "entire wheat flour," a self-explanatory name to remind you that the entire wheat berry was ground into the flour. In recent years all of the major flour companies have begun manufacturing it and usually you can find at least one brand in any supermarket. Some people feel the stone-ground offerings are better than those milled with steel blades, but the major brands all seem to taste and act about the same to me. What you find in good natural-food stores or buy from small local mills is better; what has been sitting around in bad natural-food stores is a disaster. What you grind yourself, in a home mill, is superior. Not only is it fresher and therefore more nutritious and more tasty, but also you can control the fineness of the grind. The soft wheats are sold as whole wheat pastry flour; the hard red spring and winter wheats are sold as "hard" or "bread" flours. And some stores sell mixtures of more than one kind of wheat ground together as "all-purpose" and as "bread" flours. Since the mixes vary with the mixer, about all you can do is try them until you find one you like.

What you buy when you ask for *graham flour* seems to depend on where you get it. Originally, Sylvester Graham, influenced by the Shakers, said that refined flour was "to put asunder what God joined together," and insisted that the only good flour was made from the whole kernel of the wheat. He was objecting especially to the practice of milling out the bran.

In the *Joy of Cooking,* Irma Rombauer and Marion Becker use "graham flour" and "whole grain" flour synonymously. On the other hand, James Beard, in his book on bread, discusses whole wheat flour and graham flour as two different flours, although he never makes the distinction between the two quite clear.

The people at Walnut Acres describe their graham flour as having the coarsest bran sifted out, so that it is a fine brown flour with only slightly more bran than unbleached white flour. But the people at Guistos, in San Francisco, suppliers for a number of natural-food stores, describe their graham flour as being different from other whole wheat flours because it has a very coarse grind. No wonder people get confused about flours. You pays your money and you takes your choice.

If you're buying flour, the best thing to do is concentrate on what the flour seems like to you without worrying too much about what it's called. As the General Semantics practitioners are fond of reminding us, "The word is not the thing."

Puffed wheat shows up on the shelves of health-food stores sometimes; it's expensive and not much different from the puffed wheat you can buy in the grocery store. If you're really interested in using whole grains, you probably won't be much interested in buying all the air that goes with puffed wheat.

Early stone grinder.

Rolled wheat looks a lot like rolled oats and can be used in all the same ways. You'll find it a good buy for adding variety to your granola recipes. It's nearly always sold in bulk in natural-food stores: I've never seen it in a supermarket.

Wheat germ comes either raw or toasted. Either way, make sure it's fresh because wheat germ, containing the oil of the grain, goes rancid just as unpreserved oil would. In the supermarket, wheat germ is available in vacuum-sealed jars; in natural-food stores it is commonly sold in bulk or packaged in plastic bags. Unless the wheat germ is refrigerated, you may be better off with the supermarket jars. Never, never buy bulk wheat germ that has been sitting in a big barrel in a warm store. It won't taste good and it won't be good for you.

Triticale Less Complicated

Buying triticale is less complicated than buying wheat because, so far, fewer things have been done to it. Not all natural-food stores carry triticale in all its currently available forms, and grocery stores usually don't carry it at all. If the grain grows in popularity and is improved even more with continued breeding experiments, it may become more widely sold and used in more varieties.

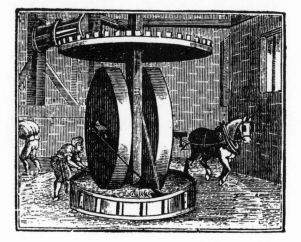

Triticale berries are slightly longer and look more shriveled than wheat berries. You should be able to find them in natural-food stores that sell wheat berries.

Triticale flakes or *rolled triticale* looks like and can be used like rolled wheat and oats. Natural-food stores that don't carry the flakes could order them for you.

Triticale flour resembles rye flour. If your natural foods store doesn't have it, you could grind your own or have it ordered. It can be used like wheat flour if you allow for the fact that its gluten is more delicate than that of wheat and requires less handling (kneading and rising) to develop.

So far I have not seen cracked triticale, but you could certainly make your own from the berries, and there may be stores somewhere offering it, since the process would not be any more complicated than is grinding it into flour.

Using Triticale

Here are a few recipes specifically for triticale. All the recipes in the Rye chapter for using rye berries would be appropriate also for triticale berries. Triticale flour can also be substituted for rye flour. When you begin thinking of substituting triticale flour for wheat flour, remember that the gluten in triticale seems to be more delicate—knead less and settle for one rising rather than two. In earlier experiments, some cooks thought triticale was as low in gluten as rye; however, more recently, the experiments of Marlene Ann Bumgarner, who wrote *The Book of Whole Grains*, suggested that the gluten was there but had to be handled more gently. My own tests bear this out. You'll find few recipes for triticale in other books, so anything you try also will be an experiment. At this point in the development of techniques for cooking with triticale, most of the wisdom is word-of-mouth.

CABBAGE
STUFFED WITH TRITICALE

2 cups water
1 cup triticale berries
1 large onion, chopped
1 pound very lean pork
   sausage
1 large cabbage
1 cup tomato juice
Salt and pepper

Bring the water to a boil and slowly stir the triticale berries, which have been rinsed, into it. (Note that this is not as much water as you usually use for cooking a cup of raw grain.)

As soon as the water is boiling again, lower the heat, cover the pan, and simmer. While the triticale is cooking, chop the onion and combine it with the sausage. Carefully remove leaves from a large head of cabbage and steam them, a few at a time, until just soft enough to bend. Cool. When the triticale has cooked about thirty minutes and all the moisture is absorbed, remove from the heat and cool. The berries should still be chewy, *not* completely tender. (If necessary, cook off remaining moisture with the lid removed for a few minutes.) Combine the cooled triticale berries with the sausage and onion and add salt and pepper.

Put a tablespoonful of the triticale-sausage mixture in the center of each cabbage leaf, fold in the sides, and shape the leaf into a roll. Fasten with a toothpick or, if you're in a hurry, just place the roll with the edge on the bottom and it will be pretty well held together by its own weight. Cover the bottom of a large baking dish with the cabbage rolls and then stack them up into layers until all the stuffing mixture is used.

Pour the tomato juice over the cabbage rolls and add water until they are covered about to the halfway point.

On top of the stove bring the contents of the casserole to a boil, cover, and put into a preheated 325° F. oven. Watch the dish and regulate heat so that the liquid is just barely bubbling. Usually this ends up being about 275° F. once everything is hot. Cook slowly for 1 to 1½ hours, or until the triticale has become tender (but not mushy) and the pork is well done and looks grey rather than pink. You may add a little more water if needed during the cooking period.

Serve the cabbage rolls as they are, or thicken the juice by stirring in one tablespoon corn starch softened in ¼ cup water and simmering and stirring until the mixture cooks clear again.

Mashed potatoes are the perfect companion for cabbage rolls to make a good country supper.

MAKES 6–8 SERVINGS

TRITICALE WITH RICE

2½ cups water
½ cup long-grain brown rice
½ cup triticale berries
¼ teaspoon salt

This is one recipe for which only triticale will do. The results are much like wild rice mixed with rice, only a lot cheaper and more nutritious. The triticale is a darker, longer, and crisper grain than the rice, and this adds appeal to the mixture.

Bring the water to a boil while you are rinsing the rice and triticale berries. Add the salt and, as soon as the water is boiling, stir in the two grains slowly, keeping the heat on high. As soon as the water begins to boil again, reduce heat to low, cover the pan and simmer from forty to sixty minutes, or until the rice and triticale are just tender. Cook off any unabsorbed moisture by removing the lid from the pan for the last few minutes of cooking. Do not overcook or you will end up with a rice/triticale porridge, which would be fine for breakfast but certainly isn't what you want to serve with vegetables and gravy at dinner.

MAKES 4 SERVINGS

TRITICALE COOKIES

1½ cups whole wheat flour
½ teaspoon baking soda
½ teaspoon salt
1 teaspoon cinnamon
⅛ teaspoon ground clove
1 cup chopped dates
1¾ cups triticale flakes
1 egg, beaten
¼ cup milk
⅓ cup oil
½ cup honey

Sift together the flour, soda, salt, and spices. Stir one large spoonful of this mixture into the chopped dates. Stir the triticale and floured dates into the dry ingredients. Mix the egg, milk, oil, and honey and pour them into the dry ingredients. Mix together thoroughly and drop dough by spoonsful onto a greased cookie sheet. Bake fifteen to twenty minutes in a 325° F. oven, or until the cookies begin to brown around the edges and are cooked through. Do not overbake, as these will burn rather easily.

Glen Millward photo

Cooking with Wheat

BOILED WHEAT BERRIES

3 to 4 cups water
1 cup whole wheat berries
¼ teaspoon salt (optional)

Long before the back-to-nature movement became fashionable, a young woman I know moved to Texas where she lived in an old house on a big ranch with little money and few possessions beyond a used piano, her guitar, and a horse. "We can't afford much," she wrote, "but lots of evenings we boil up some wheat for supper and I always think it's the best meal I've ever had." That's not just the romance of the young talking. Many an old-timer recalls cooked whole wheat as a favorite food. It's so simple you've got to wonder how we nearly lost it.

Bring the water to a rolling boil and then gradually stir in the wheat berries. Add the salt if you're using it. Reduce the heat at once, cover the pan and simmer 30 to 60 minutes over low heat, timing the cooking according to how you like your wheat. The longer cooking time produces a porridge rather like oatmeal; the shorter time keeps the grains whole and chewy. A nice compromise is to cook the wheat just until the skins begin to burst, but not until everything is mushy — usually about forty minutes. Cook off any excess moisture by removing the lid. Serve hot with maple sugar or brown sugar and milk, or with a dab of butter and no sweetener.

MAKES ABOUT 5 HALF-CUP SERVINGS

53

JUDY'S WHEAT CEREAL

½ **cup toasted wheat meal**
2 **cups cold water**
¼ **teaspoon salt (optional)**

This recipe comes from the Mormons, who seem to know more about using grains than anybody else these days. And, in the wonderful way that foods cross all kinds of social divisions, the recipe came to me from a New Jersey farmer who had transplanted herself into the heart of Pennsylvania Amish country. She buys her wheat from the Amish bins, cleans it with an electric hair dryer, and then cooks it using this Mormon recipe.

Spread cleaned whole wheat berries on a cookie sheet and toast in a 200° F. oven for about forty minutes, stirring from time to time. The lower the oven heat, the longer you must toast the grain. As Judy puts it, "Keep it in the oven until it smells toasty." Then remove the grain from the oven, cool it completely and grind it, about a cupful at a time, in your blender (or in your home flour mill) to make a coarse meal. If you use the blender, you'll get a meal with some big pieces and some little pieces of wheat all mixed together, which makes an interesting texture. This toasted and ground whole wheat keeps well in a coffee can or other tightly capped container in a cool place.

When you are ready to cook the cereal, combine the wheat meal, cold water, and salt.

Bring to a boil, reduce heat, cover the pan, and simmer for about thirty minutes. If you need more water, stir it in gently so you don't stir up a pan of glue. If the cereal seems too moist, cook it for a while with the lid off. The amount of liquid you need for cooking will depend on how much moisture was removed from the grain by toasting.

MAKES 3 SERVINGS

USING A SLOW COOKER

Whole grains can be more instant than the quickest prepared cereal if you use your slow cooker.

At bed time, put 1 cup of whole or cracked grain berries into the cooker, along with about 2¼ cups water and ¼ teaspoon salt. Set the cooker on "low" and leave it. In the morning, your breakfast is hot and waiting.

For the best nutrition and an extra special taste, it's nice to use a mixture of grains rather than just one. Cracked wheat and oats make an especially good combination.

The Rival "Crockette" is the perfect size for breakfast grain and has only a low setting, just right for the job.

You may have to experiment to get the right amount of water, depending on the dryness of your grains. Generally you can expect to use slightly less water than you would use for cooking the same grain by conventional methods because less evaporation takes place in a slow cooker.

MAKES 4 SERVINGS

Glen Millward photo

Cracked oats and wheat porridge.

WHEAT SPROUTS

¼ **cup clean raw wheat berries**

3 **cups warm water**

Wheat sprouts differ from other sprouts you may have tried, such as alfalfa or mung bean, in that the sprouted wheat has a decidedly sweet taste. Wheat sprouts are good in salads and chopped up to add to yeast breads. Making sprouts is simple. Don't bother to buy any of the fancy and expensive "sprouters" on the market because, ultimately, a plain mason jar, which you probably have already, works better.

Pick out any broken kernels from the wheat, put the berries in a quart jar, cover with the warm water and soak overnight. The next day, fasten a piece of cheesecloth on top of the jar, or use one of the screwcap-screens now being sold in natural-food stores and garden catalogs especially for the purpose, and drain away the soaking water. Hold the jar under gently running warm water and wash the grain well. Drain thoroughly. The grain will already be showing signs of sprouting. Shake the jar so the grains are scattered along one side, and put it on its side in a warm, dark place. Take a moment to wash the sprouts at least twice a day, until they reach the length you want (takes about three or four days), then rinse in cold water and refrigerate. Don't let wheat sprouts get too long, not much more than ¼ inch, because as they grow longer they develop little hair roots which look spidery and unappetizing.

MAKES 1 CUP SPROUTS

56

Whole Wheat Pasta

Making noodles with whole wheat flour takes a lot of work and either a strong arm or a pasta machine. A hand-cranked, Italian-made machine that kneads, rolls, and cuts the dough is on the market for under $50. If you want to make noodles often, it would probably be a good investment. Recently a variety of electric machines which mix the dough and then either extrude it, as for spaghetti, or push out dough ready to be cut, have become available. They seem like marvelous devices; unfortunately they all cost $200 or more. Unless you're running a restaurant, you'd have to be pretty hooked on pasta to justify that kind of expenditure.

Whole wheat pasta differs from that made with white or unbleached flour not only in taste, but also in texture because the bran is coarser than the rest of the flour and absorbs water and swells more than the rest of the flour as the noodles cook. Also, pasta you make at home will be different from what you buy, whether you use and buy whole wheat or white, because commercial pastas are made from durum or red durum wheat, which produces a firmer product, while you probably will use an all-purpose or bread wheat which you've grown or bought for a variety of uses. If you find some durum wheat, by all means try it.

Finally, homemade pasta tastes better than what you buy in the store, even if your efforts are uneven and crude, because it is so much fresher. Here are two recipes, one using unbleached white flour and the other using whole wheat flour. If you are new to making pasta, try the unbleached white recipe first, even though it is nutritionally inferior to the whole wheat, to give yourself a chance to get the hang of the process before working with the more difficult whole grain.

Grant Heilman Photography

PALE NOODLES

1½ **cups unbleached
       white flour**
Pinch salt
2   **medium eggs**

Put all but a few spoonsful of the flour in a large mixing bowl or pile it onto a smooth counter surface. Sprinkle the salt over the flour. Make a well in the flour and break the eggs into it, stirring the flour and eggs together with the fork as you do so. The mixture will be crumbly and poorly mixed, but don't worry about it. As soon as the egg is stirred in well enough not to be wet, mix the dough some more with your hands. Use as much of the reserved flour as you need to get the dough to the point where you can handle it. Proportions cannot be exact because the amount of egg the flour will absorb depends on the flour's moisture content. If you started out with too much flour, sneak a few drops of water in, but don't admit it to anybody because no noodle maker of repute has to rely on water. Once you have the egg and flour (and possibly water) pretty well mixed together, squeeze it into a ball, cover it with a damp cloth and do something else for about twenty minutes.

Glen Millward photo

Break eggs into flour and stir.

Work dough with your hands.

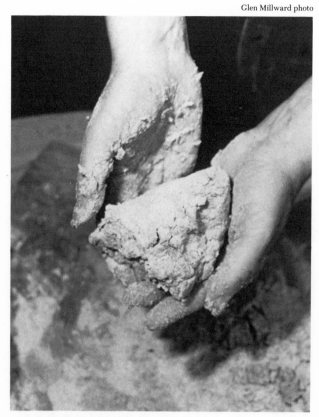

Then squeeze it into a ball.

When you get back to your lump of noodle dough, knead it for a few minutes on a lightly floured surface, adding extra flour if the dough seems sticky. You'll be surprised at how much easier the dough is to handle after its twenty-minute rest. If you are using a hand-cranked pasta machine, divide the kneaded dough into two pieces and start putting a piece through the rollers, folding it and putting it through the rollers again and again. Gradually narrow the space between the rollers to thin or "roll out" the dough. It's more likely that you'll be without a machine and rolling the dough out by hand the first few times, at least. This is easier to do if you've kneaded it thoroughly first. And, since noodle dough is very stiff, both the kneading and rolling require a lot of muscle. It's easier to work with smaller pieces and don't be ashamed to enlist the strongest arm around for this part of the job. I've seen a man who used to work in the steel mills labor over pasta dough until the veins on his arms bulged.

As you roll, dust the dough lightly from time to time with flour to prevent sticking. The thinness you strive to attain depends on what kind of pasta you're making. Some things, pot pie noodles for instance, don't need to be too thin. But others, like a fine fettucini, should be quite thin.

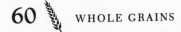

Glen Millward photo

Glen Millward photo

Cut thin layer with pasta machine.

Drop in, a few at a time.

After the dough is appropriately thin, cut it to shape with a sharp knife (or with the cutter blades if you're using a pasta machine) and allow it to dry, either on racks, towels, or hanging over chair backs, for a few minutes before cooking. You can dry the noodles completely at this point and store them as you would commercial pasta products, but you'll never equal the flavor of a freshly made, freshly cooked pasta. If you have room in your freezer, freeze any pasta you aren't planning to cook immediately.

To cook your homemade noodles, bring a huge kettleful of water to a rolling boil and drop the noodles into the boiling water a few at a time, stirring with a wooden spoon to keep them from sticking to each other. Keep the water boiling and keep an eye on the pan to make sure it doesn't boil over. Your spoon can keep the foam knocked down. Don't go far away while the pasta is boiling because it cooks much faster than the commercial kinds, in as little as four or five minutes, depending on how dry it is and how thin you've rolled it.

As soon as the pasta is just tender, pour it into a colander, mix in a dab of butter or oil to keep it from sticking to itself, and serve immediately. Do not overcook. Homemade pasta gets even more mushy than the kind you buy if overcooked.

If you've gone to this much work to produce a fine-flavored homemade noodle, don't obscure your efforts with a strong sauce the first

Glen Millward photo

Drain in a colander.

Glen Millward photo

Serve with a simple sauce.

time. Try something simple like melted butter and poppy seeds, a light clam sauce, or just a little cottage cheese and parsley mixed in. It'll taste so good you may never go to those elaborate sauces again. And it'll taste so good you'll wish you had made more.

Figure roughly ¾ cup flour plus one egg for each person you're serving. If you're going to be making a lot, you'll find it easier to handle in small batches rather than in one big lump.

MAKES 2–3 SERVINGS

WHOLE WHEAT PASTA

1 cup whole wheat flour
Pinch salt
2 eggs

The proportions differ dramatically when you're making noodles from whole wheat flour because it absorbs so much more liquid.

Proceed exactly as in the previous recipe, adding more flour if needed to keep the dough from being sticky. Be sure to allow at least one quart of water for each serving of pasta you're cooking when you get ready to boil it. This is especially important with whole wheat pasta, since it absorbs more moisture and swells more during cooking.

MAKES 2 SERVINGS

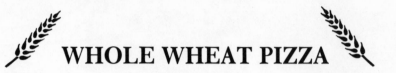

WHOLE WHEAT PIZZA

1 package active dry yeast

1¼ cups warm water (90°–105° F.)

1 tablespoon sugar

½ teaspoon salt

2 tablespoons oil

3 cups whole wheat flour

1 tablespoon olive oil

2½ cups canned tomatoes, well drained

1 clove garlic, finely minced

½ small can tomato paste

½ teaspoon oregano

Grated cheese

Toppings: sausage, mushrooms, anchovies, etc.

This recipe was born on a cross-country trip in a camper when all the kids wanted pizza and nothing but brown flour remained in the pantry. It turned out to be everybody's favorite pizza. Interestingly, a number of pizza parlors are beginning to offer whole wheat pizza and customers like it.

Dissolve the yeast in the water with the sugar. Allow to stand until the mixture bubbles, then add the salt and oil and beat in the flour gradually. Use more or less as needed to make a dough you can handle. Cover with a damp cloth for fifteen minutes, then flop the dough onto a lightly floured surface and knead thoroughly until smooth and elastic. Put the kneaded dough in a greased bowl, cover, and allow to stand in a warm place until the dough is doubled in bulk.

When the dough has doubled, punch it down and either roll it out with a rolling pin or just push it into a circle with your hands, to fit a fourteen-inch pizza pan. If you don't have a pizza pan, fit the dough onto a cookie sheet. It looks less authentic but works just as well. Oil the pan lightly before you put the dough on, and use the tablespoon of olive oil to oil the top of the dough too. The dough may still be quite springy and not want to hold its shape. Just keep pushing it back into place and don't worry if its shape isn't perfect.

To make the sauce, break up the canned tomatoes into very small pieces—almost a puree—with a fork. Drain off as much moisture as you can, then mix in the garlic, tomato paste, and oregano. Spread the sauce on the pizza, sprinkle with any kind of grated cheese you like (mozzarella or provolone would be traditional), add some toppings and bake the pizza in a 425° F. oven for about twenty minutes, or until the bread is baked through and the sauce and cheese are hot and bubbling.

The sauce for this pizza may seem almost too simple; most pizza sauces are cooked. But the uncooked sauce produces a fresh taste, reminiscent of the marvelous, lighly cooked tomato sauces for which the Italians are famous, that blends perfectly with the fuller flavor of whole wheat.

MAKES 4 SERVINGS

Glen Millward photo

BAKED BEANS WITH BULGUR

1 cup dried navy
  pea beans
1 cup coarse bulgur

---

1 medium onion,
  chopped
1 3-inch cube of salt
  pork, diced
¼ cup brown sugar
¼ cup molasses
½ teaspoon salt
1 teaspoon dry mustard
3 cups stock (or water)

I got this recipe in a class on cooking with whole grains. As Diana Robertson, the instructor, was assembling the ingredients and talking about the recipe, which she created herself, I was skeptical about it. But as it cooked it smelled better and better and when we finally sampled some she had prepared the day before, I was dumbfounded. The recipe makes what could easily be the best baked beans I've ever tasted, and the combination of wheat and beans makes a good protein.

Soak the beans overnight in cold water, or use the quick-soak method of bringing them to a boil and letting them stand in the hot water for an hour. Simmer the soaked beans until they are tender, anywhere from two to four hours depending on how dry the beans were to begin with. In a baking dish large enough to hold at least eight cups, combine the cooked beans and the bulgur. Add the chopped onion, salt pork, brown sugar, molasses, salt, and dry mustard. Cover with bean liquid, water, stock, or a combination of all three. Bake covered in a 200° F. oven for eight hours, adding more liquid from time to time if necessary to keep the beans moist enough.

MAKES 6 SERVINGS

63

BEAN SOUP WITH WHEAT

½ cup dried kidney beans
½ cup dried navy pea beans
½ cup dried baby limas
½ cup dried black-eyed peas
½ cup dried lentils
Water
2 to 3 ham hocks
1 Cornish game hen or other small fowl
1 carrot, chopped
1 large onion, chopped
2 cloves garlic, minced
1 bay leaf
½ teaspoon thyme
½ teaspoon sage
Salt
1 cup whole wheat berries
2 tablespoons sherry

Vegetarians are especially mindful of the value of combining grains and legumes to provide higher quality proteins. This recipe includes meat for flavor, but the grain-bean combination improves its stick-to-the-ribs quality even more.

Wash all the dried beans, put them in a large soup kettle, and cover with cold water. Let the beans soak overnight. Don't substitute the quick-soak method here; somehow you lose character in the soup when you do.

Next morning taste the bean soaking water. If it is bitter, drain it off and cover the beans with fresh water; if it tastes sweet simply put the pot on the stove and simmer the beans. After the beans have cooked for about one hour, add the ham hocks, Cornish hen, chopped carrot and onion, minced garlic, bay leaf, thyme, sage, and salt. Simmer about one hour more, stirring occasionally and adding water if necessary to keep the soup soupy. Add the wheat berries and simmer about forty-five minutes longer, or until the wheat is tender but still chewy. Again, add more water during the simmering if the soup gets too thick. Just before serving, season with the sherry.

MAKES 12 SERVINGS

WHOLE WHEAT BISCUITS

2 cups whole wheat flour (preferably pastry)
2 teaspoons baking powder
½ teaspoon salt
4 tablespoons oil
About ¾ cup milk

If you're accustomed to white-flour biscuits, these will take some getting used to because they're definitely more substantial. They're wonderful as a base for creamed chipped beef, tuna and peas, and other "soupy" dishes. The recipe comes from the people at Walnut Creek.

Sift the dry ingredients together. Combine the oil and the milk, then stir into the dry mixture. If the dough is very stiff (this will depend on how dry your flour was), add more milk until you have a dough/batter the right consistency to drop into greased muffin tins. Each cup should be about half full. Bake in a 400° F. oven for about twenty minutes, or until the biscuits have risen and are well browned.

MAKES 10–12 BISCUITS

Bean soup with wheat.

TABULI

2 cups boiling water
1 cup coarse bulgur
2 stalks celery, chopped
1 cucumber, peeled and diced
1 bunch green onions, chopped
3 tablespoons chopped black olives
¼ cup chopped fresh parsley
½ cup lemon juice
¼ cup olive oil
¼ cup salad oil
Romaine lettuce
1 avocado, peeled and sliced
3 tablespoons pine nuts
1 medium tomato, chopped
¼ cup cooked garbanzo beans

Tabuli has as many different spellings as bulgur, some of them amusingly phonetic—ta-boó-lee, for instance. And it has even more recipes than it has spellings. This recipe for tabuli is adapted from several good ones I've tried and contains a number of ingredients which would keep it from being authentically Middle Eastern, while leaving out the traditional mint, which no Middle Easterner would be without. Try this and then make up your own.

Pour the boiling water over the bulgur in a large mixing bowl and allow to stand for one hour. Drain and squeeze out as much of the moisture as you can with your hands. Add the chopped celery, cucumber, green onions, black olives, and parsley. Mix together gently and pour on the combination of lemon juice, olive oil, and salad oil, which have been shaken together. Mix again and refrigerate several hours or overnight.

At serving time, arrange romaine lettuce leaves on a large platter, pile the tabuli mixture in the center and garnish with the avocado, pine nuts, chopped tomato, and garbanzo beans.

MAKES 6 SERVINGS

100 PERCENT WHOLE WHEAT BREAD

1 package active dry yeast
1 tablespoon sugar
¼ cup warm water (90°–105° F.)
2 cups warm water
1 teaspoon salt
3 tablespoons oil
6 tablespoons honey
5 cups whole wheat flour
½ cup nonfat dried milk powder

Even people who normally dislike whole wheat like this bread because it is somewhat sweet and quite moist. A slice of this bread, a chunk of cheese, and an apple make a substantial lunch or breakfast.

Dissolve the yeast and sugar in the ¼ cup water and allow to stand until the mixture begins to bubble. Add the two cups warm water, salt, oil, and honey and then begin beating in the flour. When you have about half of it worked in, beat in the dried milk, a little at a time, taking care to avoid lumps. Then beat in the rest of the flour. When the mixture is shiny and pulls away from the sides of the bowl in long, elastic strings, divide it into two greased pans, 5 × 9 inches or a little smaller. For a nicely shaped loaf the dough should fill the pans by about half.

Cover them with a damp cloth and allow to rise in a warm place until nearly doubled in bulk. Bake at 400° F. for about forty-five minutes. This bread is better cool than warm.

MAKES 2 LOAVES

FRENCH-STYLE WHOLE WHEAT BREAD

4 packages active dry
  yeast
5 cups lukewarm water
  (90°–105° F.)
2 tablespoons oil
1 tablespoon honey
3 teaspoons salt
5 cups unbleached white
  flour
5 cups whole wheat flour
3 to 5 cups more
  unbleached white flour

This is one of my favorite breads. The recipe came from a cookbook put together by the Unitarian-Universalists in State College, Pennsylvania, who are a notoriously enthusiastic bunch of eaters.

Combine the yeast, water, oil, honey, and salt. Stir in the 5 cups unbleached white flour, cover the bowl, and leave it in a warm place for the mixture to bubble one to five hours. The longer it stands, the more it will take on a slight sourdough flavor.

Beat in the whole wheat flour and then gradually work in more unbleached white flour until you have a dough you can handle. Knead until smooth and put in a greased bowl to rise until at least double in bulk. If you don't feel like baking when it's ready, you can punch it down and allow it to rise a second time.

Shape the dough into five long loaves. They will be skinny because the finished loaves are only about three inches in diameter. Arrange the loaves on a greased cookie sheet, make three diagonal slashes in the top of each loaf, and brush with cold water. Put the loaves into a cold oven and turn it to warm. When you see that the bread is starting to rise, turn the oven to 400° F. and bake until the crust is brown. This takes about twenty-five minutes. For a very hard crust, brush the loaves with cold water once or twice more as they bake.

MAKES 5 SMALL LOAVES

WHOLE WHEAT PANCAKES
WITH CORNMEAL

very good

*add yogurt
vanilla, cinnamon*

1   package active dry
    yeast
¼   cup warm water
1   teaspoon sugar
2   eggs
1¼ cups milk
⅓   cup light molasses
¼   teaspoon salt
1   cup cornmeal
1   cup whole wheat
    flour

These are yeast pancakes, so no baking powder is used. They're somewhat more substantial than standard pancakes and make a wonderful showcase for freshly ground whole wheat flour.

Dissolve the yeast in the warm water with the sugar. Allow to stand about five minutes, or until the mixture begins to bubble. Stir in the eggs, half the milk, and the molasses, salt, and cornmeal. Mix well, then beat in the whole wheat flour. When smooth, stir in the rest of the milk. Allow the mixture to stand twenty to thirty minutes (or refrigerate as long as overnight) before baking. Bake on a hot, lightly greased griddle.

MAKES ABOUT 10 FIVE-INCH PANCAKES

WHOLE WHEAT SHORTBREAD

1   cup butter
½   cup sugar
Pinch salt
2½ cups sifted whole
      wheat flour

Cream together the butter and sugar. Sprinkle in the salt and stir in the flour. Mix well and chill the dough for several hours. Use a cookie press or a pastry tube to form strips, stars, bows, etc., on a lightly greased cookie sheet. Bake ten to twelve minutes in a 350° F. oven.

WHOLE WHEAT PASTRY SHELL

1 cup whole wheat flour
    (preferably pastry)
¼ teaspoon salt
⅓ cup cold butter
Ice water

Don't trust anybody who tells you it's easy to work with whole wheat pastry. I watched an instructor demonstrating how to make whole wheat pastry try three times to roll it out and finally give up and just push the dough into the pie pan with her hands. It tasted fine done that way and unless you're a genius with a rolling pin, that may be the best way to produce a whole wheat pie shell. You'll find pie shell recipes with eggs included among the ingredients and you'll find recipes calling for oil rather than shortening, but this recipe, which is about the same as most recipes for white-flour pie shells, is more or less standard.

Mix the flour and salt in a bowl and cut in the butter until it is the size of small peas. With a fork, toss the mixture while sprinkling cold water over it, ½ tablespoonful at a time. Use only enough water to hold the ingredients together and make the dough manageable. With your hands, shape the dough into a ball. Try not to handle it too much, but don't be afraid to squeeze it enough to make the particles stick together. Now, if you're going to try rolling it, refrigerate the dough for about thirty minutes. Otherwise, pat it into a nine-inch pie pan with your hands, pressing the edges into the traditional fluted rim. For rolling, lightly flour a piece of waxed paper, mash the ball of dough into a circle, flour the dough's top lightly, and cover with another piece of waxed paper. Roll from the center toward the edges, lifting up the pin as you get to the edge each time and checking to see that the waxed paper is not sticking. For a baked shell, bake at 400° F. for twelve minutes, or until the pastry begins to turn a delicate brown. For an unbaked shell, proceed as you would with any other pastry.

MAKES 1 NINE-INCH SHELL

APPLESAUCE CAKE

½ cup butter

½ cup honey

1 egg

1 cup applesauce (unsweetened)

1 cup raisins

¼ cup chopped nuts

¼ cup toasted, shredded coconut

2 cups whole wheat flour (preferably pastry)

1 teaspoon soda

1 teaspoon cinnamon

1 teaspoon allspice

½ teaspoon salt

½ teaspoon baking powder

½ teaspoon ground cloves

This is a moist, spicy cake, heavier than those made with white flour. It really doesn't need frosting.

Cream the butter and honey and egg until the mixture is smooth. Stir in the applesauce, raisins, nuts, and coconut. Sift the dry ingredients together into the applesauce mixture and stir with a wooden spoon until well blended. Pour the batter into a greased and floured nine-inch layer pan or into three small (about 3 × 6 inches) loaf pans and bake at 375° F. twenty to forty minutes, or until cake tests done. The baking time will vary with the size of your pans.

MAKES 6–8 SERVINGS

WALNUT ACRES
WHOLE WHEAT COOKIES

½ cup butter

1 cup brown sugar

1 egg

½ teaspoon vanilla

2 cups whole wheat flour

2 teaspoons baking powder

½ teaspoon salt

¼ cup milk

Raisins or nuts (optional)

Cream together the butter and sugar, then beat in the egg and vanilla. Sift together the dry ingredients and add them alternately with the milk, beginning and ending with dry ingredients. When all ingredients are throughly mixed, drop the batter by teaspoonsful onto a greased cookie sheet. If you wish, press a raisin or nut onto the top of each cookie. Bake eight to twelve minutes in a 375° F. oven. Be careful that the cookies do not burn. Burned whole wheat tastes awful!

A Final Word About Whole Wheat Recipes

One could easily fill an entire book with recipes for whole wheat flour alone. When you think about it, our ancestors didn't use any other kind of wheat flour before the days of refining. This means that all the white-flour recipes we tend to take as standard now were actually rather recently developed. Therefore, *undeveloping* them, returning them to whole wheat, shouldn't be difficult. And in fact, it isn't. You'll find some rather elaborate instructions in some cookbooks for substituting whole wheat for white flours. They go into detail about increasing shortening and liquids by percentages and so on, but you really need not get that involved. Just try changing the white flour in some of your favorite recipes to whole wheat flour, remembering that because of the bran, which absorbs moisture, you *may* have to put in a little extra liquid. If you are working with a favorite recipe, you already know how it should look. As you experiment, simply try for something that looks about the same, using whole wheat flour. Fool around with it until it suits you. After all, no recipe is sacred.

WHEAT BERRY MEASUREMENTS

1 pound wheat	=	2½ cups
0.6 cup of wheat	=	1 cup of flour
1 cup wheat	=	1 quart wheat sprouts

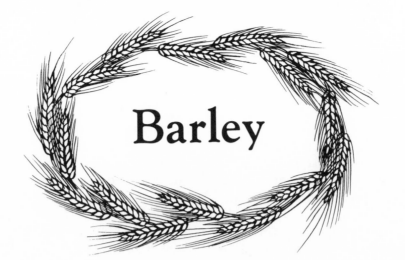

Barley

Practically everything about barley depends. When you plant depends on what kind you grow; the variety you grow depends on where you live and what you want it for. Even the cooking time depends on how much it's been refined.

Although barley, believed to be man's oldest cultivated grain, has adapted to virtually every climate and location, and appears in at least 300 different varieties, it isn't popular as food for humans in the United States, where about half of all that's grown is used for animal food (particularly cows and pigs) and 30 percent more is for malting. In some countries barley is a staple. The Japanese grow it intensively in small fields, often following a rice crop, planting the rice in furrows and the barley on the ridge of the furrow. As recently as the late 1950s such fields were tended mostly with hand labor, indicating that barley can indeed be a garden crop.

Growing Barley

The same properties that have made barley one of man's most widely adapted grains make it relatively easy to grow. And no matter where you live, you'll probably find fields of barley in the rural areas. Confronted with the tremendous number of varieties available, you may decide the hardest part of growing barley is deciding what kind to plant.

The varieties fall into two groups: two-row for malting and animal feed, and six-row, pre-ferred for eating. These figures refer to the number of rows of grain on the head of the stalk. Further, you can plant a "bearded" barley, which has an awn on the head, or you can plant a "naked" barley, which has no beard. Within these categories, new hybrids are being developed almost continuously. As if that weren't enough confusion, you have to decide whether to plant your barley in the spring (more common) or fall, and choose a variety accordingly.

Fortunately, the solution to all these decisions is simpler than the description of the problem. You plant whatever varieties are most common in your area. If you can't consult a farmer, get the local Extension agent or Soil Conservation Service representative or farm store salesman.

Generally, barley behaves enough like wheat for you to figure on planting it in the fall if you live where farmers grow winter wheat and in the spring if you live where they plant spring wheat. Although barley is fairly hardy, planting it in the fall is not recommended where winter temperatures average much below freezing.

Having decided what kind of barley to plant and when to plant it, you'll have to find seed. The obvious answer seems to be to buy it from a local farm store, but often these stores sell only in the large quantities used by farmers who plant many acres. You won't need anywhere near that much. You can harvest about one bushel of barley from 1,000 square feet and you'll need about 2.75 pounds of barley to seed that area. If one bushel of barley doesn't sound like much to you, consider that one cup of raw barley cooks up to serve six people generously and that most soup recipes call for only about ⅓ cup raw grain, even for a big pot of soup.

Smaller quantities of seed are beginning to be offered in some of the garden seed catalogs, a trend which may grow with the increasing interest in growing grains on a small scale. For specific catalogs and addresses, consult the Appendix. Another way to get a small amount of seed is to buy it from a farmer in the area. Out of his large planting, he'll hardly miss two or three pounds and he might be a good source of information on what to expect from your crop.

Preparing the Soil

Once you have seed, preparing the ground, planting, and cultivating progress much as with any other garden crop. Work the soil until it is in good tilth and weed-free. A pH of 7 to 8 is about right. Barley tolerates alkaline conditions but is sensitive to acidity, so if you are in doubt, add a little lime. The soil should be fertile, but be careful about adding nitrogem. Too high a nitrogen content encourages stalk growth but reduces the amount of grain those stalks produce, just as too much nitrogen can give you tomato plants with beautiful foliage and few tomatoes or huge carrot tops with tiny roots.

Typically, in the United States, you see barley sown in solid blocks, usually drilled, and on the small scale you can accomplish this by broadcasting the seed, either by hand or with a hand-cranked seeder. Then go over the area with a rake to scratch the seed into the ground. With this method, the barley, which sprouts and begins to show green in as few as three or four days if moisture and warmth are adequate, chokes out most weeds.

The Japanese grow some barley in rows. In Arizona, research has shown that this method produces higher yield per pound of seed, with rows fourteen inches across, and with space between rows for cultivating. The size and shape of your garden plot may determine whether you broadcast or plant in rows. Either way, don't cover the seed more than a skinny inch.

After planting you shouldn't have much to do with your barley crop, unless you are irrigating, except to pull out any overpowering weeds, for the next sixty days or so. Winter barley ripens about sixty days after growth begins to show in the spring; spring barley ripens about seventy days after you sow it. A long-time farmer describes her typically seat-of-the-pants test for knowing when it's time to harvest barley or any grain in this way, "I wait till it looks brown, then I break a head off its stalk and rub it around in my hands. If the grain rubs out easily, I bite it. If it bites hard, it's ready."

Another test is to dent a kernel with your thumbnail. If the dent doesn't disappear, the grain is past the milky stage and ready to harvest. The straw will be dry at this time.

Harvesting

After your first harvest you'll be able to devise your own tests and you can supplement your judgment by consulting with your local Extension agent or Soil Conservation Service representative. Or watch to see when local farmers begin their harvests.

Assuming you've planted only a small amount of barley, the easiest — indeed the only — way to harvest is by hand, with a sickle or scythe. The sickle, having a short handle, is probably easier for a novice to use and is more suited to handling in a small space. (For a detailed description of a good way to cut and bundle grains, see the chapter on wheat.) Leave the bundles in the field for a few days to season, then thresh it. Even a little rain won't hurt.

Threshing

If you are threshing only a small amount, the easiest way is probably the old method of holding a bundle at a time upside down over a barrel and banging it back and forth against the

Old Sturbridge Village photo by Donald F. Eaton

Flailing grain at Old Sturbridge Village.

sides. This is slow, however, and for handling large quantities you may want to try a flail, or the thresher described in the wheat chapter.

The threshed barley will be mixed with chaff and bits of dirt which must be winnowed out. The time-honored way to do this is to pour the grain repeatedly from one container to another in a stiff breeze until the grain is acceptably clean. In olden days a strong wind or antique fanning mill did the job; more recent innovations range from electric fans and hair dryers to commercial seed cleaners. And when all else fails, you can still pick out offending bits of dirt by hand.

How you store the cleaned barley depends on how much you have. See the description for storing wheat and follow it.

However you store it, barley requires some further treatment before you can use it for anything but animal feed. The hull on barley is so tough that cooking it long enough to get it chewable takes forever and in the process destroys nutrients.

Removing the Hull

In commercial operations the hull is removed in a series of steps called "pearling." The pearler consists of abrasive disks that revolve within a perforated cylinder to grind the hulls, germ, and bran from the kernel. The cylinder is designed to keep the barley turning so the hull is removed uniformly. The barley is pearled for a few minutes, transferred to a screen to sift off the hulls, and then the process is repeated. After three pearlings all the hull and most of the bran have been removed, leaving what is called "pot barley." After a total of five or six pearlings that remove all the bran and hull and also most of the embryo, or germ, the grain is called "pearled barley." Barley flour is sifted from the residue of the fourth, fifth, and sixth pearlings or milled from the pearled grains.

On the small homestead scale, all you really need is a way to get enough hull off the barley so that you can cook it tender. If you don't need more than a few cups at a time, whirling the barley in a blender and then doing a small-scale winnowing in front of an electric fan or with a hair dryer may be the simplest. You can buy a hand-operated or an electric-powered pearler, but unless you plan to use bushels and bushels of barley, it hardly seems worth the cost.

Buying Barley

If all this sounds like more work than you want for a few barley casseroles and a pot of soup, here's how to buy barley. Having read the previous description of what happens to grain sold as "pearled" you probably will want to avoid that most highly refined barley and look, instead, for "pot barley." Your best chances of finding pot barley are in good natural-food stores, but don't assume you've got pot barley just because you found barley there. Some stores don't put any label on the bin; check with the store manager before you assume anything. If you can't find pot barley anywhere, choose the brownest of what you can find, since that will be an indication that more hull is left. Occasionally you'll see unhulled barley for sale. It really is not a good buy unless you're prepared to try to knock off some of the hull yourself or else chew on a mouthful of barley for a very long time before swallowing.

Using Barley

As you check to see what is available, you'll discover that all barley does not look alike. It varies in shades of brown, depending on how completely it's been refined, and it varies considerably in grain size. Interestingly, no matter how it looks, all cooked barley tastes about the same. It is probably the most bland grain grown, milder even than rice. This blandness has made it a popular ingredient for baby food and, in flour form, a wheat substitute for people with allergies. Barley flour contains no gluten, the substance in wheat flour which makes it stretchy and elastic when you knead it. This limits its uses.

If you have a flour mill, you can grind some of your purchased or homegrown barley into flour, but unless you are buying the mill for other grains as well, you may be better off buying barley flour, since you are not apt to use it in large quantities. The flour is available in most natural-food stores and some supermarkets; cracked barley (often called grits) is often found, and cooked for breakfast cereal.

A use for barley more common than making flour is malting. Commercially, beer makers use specific varieties for malting, but any barley can be malted. It's simply a process of soaking, sprouting, and drying the grain to produce the malt. Brewing beer at home is a tricky process which tends to produce inconsistent results, and the malting process, without a closely controlled environment, is even more touchy. If you have the energy and inclination to malt your own barley and brew your own beer, consult one of the many specialized books devoted to the process.

Cooking with Barley

Barley deserves more culinary attention than it's had. Although it is not the most nutritious of the grains, barley has a pleasant flavor which combines well with stronger flavors. Perhaps the most familiar use for barley is in soups. Even commercial soup companies sell a beef-with-barley soup, and the famous Scotch broth is basically a lamb and barley soup. But barley is good in hot casseroles and cold salads, too. Used alone, it makes a nice substitute for potatoes, noodles, and rice. Mixed with other grains and served with a vegetable topping, it makes a substantial meal.

BASIC STEAMED BARLEY

1 cup raw barley
3 cups water

To cook basic steamed barley, simply add it slowly to boiling water — one cup raw barley to three cups water — reduce the heat to low, cover the pan, and simmer until the grain is tender and the moisture absorbed. This takes from forty-five to sixty minutes, depending on how old the barley is and how much hull has been removed. If the barley seems done and too much liquid remains, remove the lid and cook off what liquid you don't want. If the liquid is gone before the barley is done, add a little water. If you double the basic recipe, don't quite double the amount of liquid. Hold back about one-half cup until you see whether it will be needed.

MAKES 3 CUPS

BARLEY WATER

1 tablespoon barley flour
2 tablespoons cold water
2 cups water
⅛ teaspoon salt

This recipe appeared in Mrs. Simon Kander's *Settlement Cookbook* in 1931, in a chapter devoted to preparing baby food. We include it here more as a novelty than a practical recipe, but having seen some of the powdered drinks people give babies, perhaps we should recommend barley water as a substitute, for babies with upset stomachs.

Mix the barley flour with the two tablespoons cold water, making a paste. When it is smooth, add the two cups water and salt. Boil in a double boiler for thirty minutes. Add clear spring water to replace what has cooked off so that you end up with two cups. Barley water may be kept several days in a cool place.

MAKES 1 PINT

SIMPLE BARLEY PILAF

1 cup raw barley
2 to 3 tablespoons butter
or oil
2½ to 3 cups hot liquid
(water or stock)

Sauté the grain briefly in the hot fat, stirring until each grain of barley is covered with fat and shows faint signs of beginning to brown. Add the hot liquid, bring to a boil, then lower heat, cover pan and simmer about forty-five minutes, or until barley is tender and moisture is absorbed. If the barley is tender before all the liquid has been used, lift the lid and simmer off the excess moisture before serving.

MAKES 3 CUPS

BARLEY CREAM SOUP

1 carrot, grated
1 onion, chopped
1 leek, chopped
2 stalks celery, chopped
3 tablespoons chopped
parsley
1 tablespoon butter
5 cups chicken stock
½ teaspoon salt
¼ teaspoon pepper
½ cup raw barley
1 cup sliced mushrooms
1 tablespoon butter or
chicken fat
1 tablespoon sherry
½ cup cream
2 tablespoons minced
chives

Sometimes, in earlier years, barley cream soups were served to invalids. If you are cooking for a sick person, this isn't the soup to settle an unhappy stomach, but if you're trying to tempt a faltering appetite, or warm a cold worker, this is your soup.

Sauté the carrot, onion, leek, celery, and parsley in one tablespoon butter until soft, then add the stock and seasonings and bring to a boil. Add the barley. Reduce heat and simmer, *uncovered*, over low heat for one hour. Meanwhile, sauté the mushrooms in one tablespoon butter and season them with the sherry. When the barley is done, mix the mushrooms and cream into the hot soup and serve sprinkled with the chives.

MAKES 6–8 SERVINGS

CREAM OF VEGETABLE-BARLEY SOUP

1 carrot, chopped
1 onion, chopped
1 or 2 shallots, minced
1 celery rib with leaves, chopped
1 tablespoon butter
5 cups chicken stock
½ teaspoon salt
½ cup raw barley
¼ cup nonfat dry milk
½ cup whole milk
1 cup cooked mixed vegetables

This recipe is not quite as rich and elaborate as the previous one and is probably much better for you.

Sauté the carrot, onion, shallot, and celery in the butter in your soup kettle. Add the chicken stock and salt and bring to a boil. Slowly stir in the barley, reduce the heat to low, cover the kettle, and simmer the soup until the barley is tender, about fifty minutes. Meanwhile, mix the nonfat dry milk into the whole milk and refrigerate. Lightly steam whatever vegetables you plan to use (you can use leftovers if they are in good condition) and set them aside. When the barley is tender, stir the milk mixture and vegetables into it and reheat, but do not boil. This is good served with bacon bits and mild, chopped raw onion on top.

MAKES 6–8 SERVINGS

Glen Millward photo

BEEF WITH VEGETABLES AND BARLEY SOUP

1 **pound beef chuck cut in chunks**
1 **tablespoon butter**
1 **onion, chopped**
2 **celery ribs, chopped**
2 **carrots, chopped**
1 **bay leaf**
½ **teaspoon salt**
6 **cups stock (beef, chicken or vegetable)**
¼ **cup tomato puree**
⅓ **cup raw barley**

This is a good stick-to-your-ribs soup which can be made early in the day, or even early in the week, and reheated later. It's one of the few recipes that works in a slow cooker as well as on top of the stove without producing a gooey mass of barley.

Remove as much fat as you can from the beef. Brown the beef in the butter and remove from the pan. Lightly sauté the onion, celery, and carrots in the same fat. Return the meat to the pan and add the bay leaf, salt, stock, and tomato puree. Bring everything to a boil, gradually stir in the barley, reduce the heat to low, cover the pan tightly, and cook until meat and barley are very tender—about two hours. (In the slow cooker, cooking time will be six to eight hours on low and you have to add the barley without bringing all the ingredients to a boil. It helps to use boiling stock if you do it this way.)

If the beef seems too fatty to cut away most of it, brown and simmer the meat a day ahead. Refrigerate and then remove the solidified fat. If you proceed this way, pick up the recipe instructions again by sautéing the vegetables in a small amount of butter and simmer everything only about one hour.

MAKES 6–8 SERVINGS

SCOTCH BROTH

2 pounds lamb shanks or neck bones

1 tablespoon oil

8 to 10 cups water

2 carrots, diced

2 turnips, diced

1 large onion, chopped

¼ cup raw barley

1 tablespoon tomato paste

1 teaspoon salt

If you're looking for "the authentic recipe," there's no such thing as scotch broth. As with borscht, there are nearly as many different recipes as there are pots of soup. The only ingredients absolutely standard in scotch broth are lamb and barley, so adjust the ingredients to suit your own idiosyncracies and invent yet another recipe for scotch broth.

Remove any visible fat from the lamb and then brown the meat in the oil in a deep kettle. If the shanks or neck bones don't seem to have a lot of meat on them, you may want to use more than two pounds. After browning the meat, pour off the oil and add enough hot water to cover the meat. Bring to a boil, lower heat, and cover the pot. Simmer two to three hours, or until the meat is very tender. Cool and then refrigerate until the fat rises to the top and is firm enough to lift off.

Pick the meat from the bones and cut any large pieces into bite size. Return to the heat, bring to a simmer again, and add the carrots, turnips, onion, barley, tomato paste, and salt. Simmer gently about an hour, until the barley is done. If you prefer crisp soup vegetables, don't add them until about twenty minutes before the barley should be tender. If your soup seems too thick, add water; if it seems too soupy, simmer with the lid off for a while.

MAKES 6–8 SERVINGS

HUNGARIAN BARLEY-BEAN STEW

2 cups cooked great northern beans (about 1 cup dry)

3 cups liquid from cooking beans

½ cup raw barley

1 carrot, chopped

1 turnip, peeled and chopped

½ green pepper, chopped

1 small tomato, chopped

½ teaspoon salt

1 heaping teaspoon paprika

1 small kielbasa sausage

Extra water as needed

This recipe is one you will wonder about as you read it. In fact you may feel skeptical about it right up to the moment you taste the results, but it's one of the most delicious of all the barley dishes. The idea for it came from a recipe Margaret and Ancel Keys included in their cook book, *The Benevolent Bean*. In its original form it turned out too gooey, so I fooled around to get something more to my taste. This is the result.

Put the cooked beans, which should be tender but not falling apart, into a kettle with the bean liquid or water. Bring to a boil and gradually stir in the barley. Lower heat, cover pan, and simmer gently while you prepare the vegetables. When they are ready, add them to the kettle, along with the salt and paprika, and continue simmering until the barley is nearly tender, adding water if necessary to keep the mixture soupy. The total cooking time for the barley should be no more than forty-five minutes. It probably won't be completely tender by then, but that's all right.

Cut the kielbasa into chunks, slitting the casing lengthwise as well. Brown the sausage lightly in a skillet and drain off all fat. Pour the barley-bean mixture into a baking dish, top with the browned sausage, and bake, covered, in a 350° F. oven for thirty minutes.

About ten minutes before the baking time is up, check the casserole to see if you want more liquid. Add water if necessary. This depends on how moist you like your casseroles, but both barley and beans have an astonishing ability to absorb water long after you'd expect it.

MAKES 6 GENEROUS SERVINGS

85

Barley, ready for harvest.

BAKED BARLEY

1   cup raw barley
¼   cup chopped parsley
1   shallot, minced
¼   cup butter
½   to 1 cup sliced
     mushrooms
3   cups chicken stock or
     broth
½   teaspoon salt

This simple casserole dish is better as a side dish than as an entrée.

In a heavy skillet sauté the barley, parsley, and shallot in the butter, but do not brown. As soon as the barley grains are heated and coated with the butter, put the mixture into a baking dish and quickly sauté the mushrooms in the same skillet without adding any more fat. Put the mushrooms on top of the barley in the baking dish and add most, but not all, of the stock (which should be hot). Stir in the salt, but if you're using a salted canned broth, taste first because extra salt may not be necessary. Reserve about ½ cup of the stock until you see how much the grain absorbs while baking. Bake covered at 350° F. for one hour, adding reserved stock if necessary.

MAKES 6–8 SERVINGS

PINE NUT–BARLEY CASSEROLE

½   cup pine nuts
6   tablespoons butter
1   cup raw barley
1   medium onion,
     chopped
⅓   cup chopped parsley
¼   cup chopped green
     onion
3½ to 4 cups chicken
     stock
¼   teaspoon salt

This recipe is similar to the one before except for the addition of a few more ingredients. Comparing the two recipes should give you a good sense of how to improvise with whatever ingredients you happen to have on hand when you want to make a barley casserole.

In a heavy skillet, sauté the pine nuts in the butter. Remove them from the pan as soon as they are lightly browned, leaving the butter in the pan to sauté the barley, onion, parsley, and green onion. Mix all the sautéed ingredients in a baking dish and pour three cups of hot stock over the mixture. Add the salt if needed, but if you used canned broth you probably won't need additional salt. Bake, *uncovered*, in a 375° F. oven for about one hour and ten minutes, or until the barley is tender, adding additional stock as necessary.

MAKES 6–8 SERVINGS

ORIENTAL-STYLE BARLEY

1 recipe baked barley or pine nut-barley casserole
or
At least 2 cups leftover cooked barley

2 to 3 tablespoons oil

1 cup sliced raw broccoli
or
1 cup whole raw snow peas (depending on season)

1 cup thinly sliced celery

1 cup sliced green onion

1 cup coarsely chopped raw spinach

½ cup chicken stock (or part stock and part mushroom-soaking water)

2 tablespoons minced fresh ginger root (optional)

2 dried Chinese mushrooms, soaked and chopped (optional)

1 tablespoon cornstarch

2 tablespoons cold water

1 tablespoon soy sauce

Chinese sesame oil (optional)

This recipe was first devised as a way to use leftover barley casserole, but it's so good that it's worth the effort of baking a casserole full of barley.

If you are using leftover barley, warm it gently on top of the stove at low or in a double boiler. If you are baking a casserole specifically for this recipe, have it ready to serve before you begin to cook the vegetables.

A wok is good for stir-frying, but a heavy large skillet works well, too. Heat the oil in the skillet or wok until it is very hot but not smoking. Add the broccoli or snow peas and stir over high heat until coated with oil and shiny green. The vegetable will still be mostly raw. Stir in the celery and cook a minute more. Add the green onion and finally the spinach. Stir everything together briefly and add the stock. If you like saucy vegetables, increase the stock to ¾ cup and heap up the spoonful of cornstarch thickener, when you add it later, to compensate.

Stir in the minced ginger and Chinese mushrooms if you're using them.

If you have been doing all this over high heat, the mixture should begin to boil almost at once. When it does, stir in the cornstarch which has been softened with the two tablespoons water and the soy sauce. Lower heat and continue cooking and stirring only until the sauce, which will be cloudy after you add the cornstarch mixture, has become clear again. Season with a few drops of sesame oil, if you like it, and serve over the hot barley.

MAKES 4–6 SERVINGS

BARLEY SALAD

1   **recipe basic steamed barley (three cups)**

1   **carrot, chopped**

1   **green pepper, chopped**

¼   **mild onion, chopped fine**

8   **radishes, sliced thin**

2   **tablespoons minced parsley**

DRESSING

½   **cup vegetable oil (part olive oil if you like it)**

2   **tablespoons cider vinegar**

1   **tablespoon lemon juice**

¼   **teaspoon salt**

¼   **teaspoon dried dill weed**

When the barley is just done, turn off the heat and remove the lid from the pan. Allow the barley to stand about twenty minutes to cool and dry out slightly. *Do not stir during this time.* Stirring tends to make the grain pasty. When the barley has cooled, turn it gently into a bowl that holds at least six cups and refrigerate.

Meanwhile, chop the vegetables and add them to the barley about an hour before serving time. Then pour dressing (see below) over all, mix carefully but thoroughly, then return to refrigerator.

To serve, surround the barley with big leaves of romaine or leaf lettuce and provide a big spoon so everyone can take a generous helping. This salad is so substantial that, served with a cup of soup or a bit of cheese, it makes a meal. Whether you serve it as a main dish or a side dish, it deserves attention as a separate course and its own good-sized plate at each place.

MAKES ABOUT 6 SERVINGS

90

Buckwheat

With buckwheat there's no in between. You either love it or you hate it. Its flavor is the strongest of any of the grains and its color the darkest. (Purists will tell you the cereal grains are grasses, while buckwheat is in the buckwheat or rhubarb family, and not a grass, but that's hard to take seriously when you're busy threshing it.)

Unless you're a fanatic who wants buckwheat cakes every day of the year, you may not be interested in growing buckwheat for the little flour you'll use. However, it's also a useful crop for green manuring. It rots easily and will choke out quack grass and other weeds because it grows so fast. Some beekeepers like it because the plant produces flowers for thirty days or more, even while some of its seeds are mature, but buckwheat honey has the same strong flavor as the flour and is not to everyone's taste. The plant depends on bees for pollination.

Opinions over the years have varied as to whether buckwheat is good or bad for you. It is rich in B vitamins and in lysine, one of the amino acids. One old text observed that buckwheat caused the "insides to be fevered" resulting in "eruptions of the skin." Since this was written this rash has been pinpointed as an allergic reaction to buckwheat protein. Probably the way to handle such conflicting opinions is to eat buckwheat if it appeals to you and let it go if not; forget its medicinal qualities.

Growing Buckwheat

Buckwheat will grow in almost any soil. Because of this, some farmers, intent on getting *some* return from the land, sow it where other crops are failing and nothing else will grow. But agriculturalists say this is a bad practice, unless you plow the buckwheat under, because buckwheat takes a lot out of the soil as it grows, and in harvesting it, you deplete a poor area even more. So, having acknowledged that if you insist, you *can* grow buckwheat anywhere, let's consider its best growing conditions.

Buckwheat does best in a fairly sandy, fast-draining soil, worst on heavy, wet soil, and though it responds well to being fertilized with manure low in nitrogen and potash, it likes extra phosphorus.

Buckwheat is a cool-weather crop; its flowers tend to wither in hot weather, so it should be planted late enough to keep the majority of blossoms from flowering during the hottest part of the summer, but early enough to mature before the first heavy frost kills it. It blooms five to six weeks after planting, and, depending on the variety you plant, needs ten to twelve weeks to mature. This means, in the Northeast, where buckwheat is grown commercially, that it is planted in the last week in June. Those planning to grow it as a green manure crop, and to till it

91

under, can plant it from spring to mid-summer. It germinates best in a warm soil.

Preparing the Seedbed

Prepare the seedbed as you would for any other garden crop. Some experiments in the early 1900s showed that buckwheat plants grew larger in plots where the seedbed was prepared early in the spring and worked again just before seeding instead of in plots worked only at planting time. Apparently weeds use up nutrients in the soil during the early spring period if allowed to run free. This means you'll probably get a better crop if you can plow or till the strip where you're going to plant buckwheat as early in the spring as the ground can be worked—about the same time you're planting peas. Then, at planting time, work the ground again lightly, incorporating whatever fertilizer you intend to use.

Some gardeners use buckwheat as a green manure crop, planting it after they have tilled under an early crop such as peas.

Planting the Seed

Broadcast the seed at the rate of three to four pecks (a peck weighs twelve pounds) per acre. That figures out to about one pound per 1000 square feet. After broadcasting, rake, till, or harrow the seed in, and you're done. An ideal depth for the seed is ¾ inch. Buckwheat germinates rapidly, not giving weeds much of a chance to develop, and is pretty much free of insect and fungus problems. It grows two to five feet in height, has a single stem with branches, and its green to red stem turns brown as the plant matures. A reddish stem is a sign of a poor crop for seed.

Since the buckwheat plant continues flowering even after early flowers have gone to seed, you may wonder when it should be harvested. Usually it is harvested when the largest number of seeds are ripe, before the first killing frost. If birds and hard winds aren't bothering your crop too much, just figure on getting in the buckwheat a week or so before the usual first frost in your area, without worrying too much about what percentage of the seeds are ripe. Figure on harvesting about thirty-three pounds per 1000 square feet if you have a good crop, and maybe half that the first year when you are learning to grow and harvest it.

Buckwheat shatters easily, dropping the seed to the ground before you can thresh it, so try to cut it on a damp day or early in the morning when dew is still on the stalks. Do not haul the cut grain inside right after cutting because the stalks will still be green and full of moisture. Piled up inside they could heat up and create spontaneous combustion, burning down your shed. Instead, after cutting the buckwheat with a sickle or scythe (see the chapter on wheat for a detailed description of cutting grains), tie it into bundles and allow it to dry, shocked, in the field, until the straw is brown and has lost most of its moisture. Then put the bundles gently into a cart or wagon to haul them in for threshing.

Another method is to allow the buckwheat to stand in the field until frost has killed the stalks and the seeds have dried, then cut it promptly and finish the drying process under cover. Some people think you lose more of the grain to shattering (as you cut) and birds this way. What you lose may not matter very much and the way to decide when you should do it is probably according to when you can get around to it. To check on the ripeness of the seeds, or to harvest a small amount, strip it off the stalk with your hands. The seeds, brown to black when ripe, and shaped like beechnuts, will drop into your hands easily when the crop is ready for harvesting.

Threshing

Threshing buckwheat is easy. The grains fall freely from the heads. Hold the bundles upside down over a large barrel and bang the grain heads back and forth against the inside of the barrel. Later, you can dump the straw back on the garden for mulch; it rots faster than oat or wheat straw. Chickens will delight in hunting through the straw for seeds; they can eat the seeds, hulls and all.

Before you can grind the buckwheat, it will have to be winnowed, to remove the bits of chaff and dirt from the grain. Since you'll probably use only small quantities at a time, you can pour the buckwheat from one container to another in a stiff wind or in front of an electric fan. Hand pick any bits of chaff that remain.

Whether you store the buckwheat before or after winnowing, keep it in a clean, tight container such as a lard can, in a cool, dry place. Insect infestation is not a problem. Grind flour shortly before using, or store some in an airtight container in your refrigerator.

Buying Buckwheat

Unless you know someone who is raising it, buckwheat in whole grain might be hard to buy, but groats (hulled buckwheat broken into pieces) and flour are surprisingly easy to find.

Almost any natural-food store and many supermarkets as well carry a variety of buckwheat products of good quality. As with any grain, try to find a store with high turnover where the flour is stored in a cool place.

As you shop around, you will find that the flour varies from a grayish white to almost black in color, depending on how much of the hull has been left in. The darker the color, the more roughage there is and the stronger the taste of the flour.

Groats are sold as fine, medium, or coarse, depending on how they are ground. The coarser grinds look like pieces of triangles. About the only difference among the different grinds is in

cooking time. (Incidentally, any cracked grain is technically called groats. Perhaps the reason you hear the term usually used for buckwheat is that people who know don't want to end up having to deal with tongue twisters like "oats groats.")

You can use your blender or food processor to crack buckwheat enough to use it as groats, though you may want to remove some of the bitter hulls by hand after grinding. To make flour you can use your home mill and then control the color and flavor of your flour by sifting out some of the hulls. If standard sifters aren't fine enough to remove as much of the hull as you want taken out, try a fine-mesh sieve and work the flour through it with a wooden spoon. This is tedious, but you won't be needing much, so the time it takes won't be excessive.

Using Buckwheat

You could try boiling up the whole grain of buckwheat to eat as a cereal, but because of its tough hull, which carries the most bitter flavor, you'd probably end up with a potage even Esau wouldn't eat.

Buckwheat is used mostly in pancakes. The flour can be included in other bread recipes, but few recipes suggest it, probably because of buckwheat's distinctive flavor. Its other major use is as groats or kasha—common in Middle Eastern, Jewish, and Russian cooking. Although kasha has an exotic foreign ring, buckwheat cakes, along with lots of maple syrup and breakfast sausage, were a favorite food of early Americans. Many people still think that's the best way to enjoy buckwheat.

SIMPLE BUCKWHEAT PANCAKES

1 cup buckwheat flour
1 cup unbleached white flour
1 teaspoon salt
1 tablespoon baking powder
¼ cup honey
2 cups milk
2 eggs
⅓ cup oil

Sift together the dry ingredients; beat together the liquids. Pour the liquid mixture into the dry ingredients and stir gently until everything is mixed, but do not try to beat out all the lumps.

Bake the pancakes on a lightly greased, medium-hot griddle, turning once when bubbles begin to appear on the unbaked side.

MAKES 4–6 SERVINGS

SOURDOUGH BUCKWHEATS

½ cup sourdough starter
1 cup unbleached white flour
1 cup buckwheat flour
2 cups warm water (90°–105° F.)
2 eggs, beaten
2 tablespoons molasses or honey
½ teaspoon salt
½ teaspoon baking powder
3 tablespoons melted butter
½ teaspoon baking soda dissolved in 1 tablespoon water

Mix together the starter, flours, and water in a large bowl and beat well. Cover the bowl and allow to stand overnight in a warm place. When ready to bake the pancakes, stir in the beaten eggs, honey, salt, baking powder, and melted butter. Finally, stir in the baking soda dissolved in water. Bake on a lightly greased, moderately hot griddle, turning once after bubbles begin to form on the unbaked side.

MAKES 4–6 SERVINGS

YEAST BUCKWHEAT CAKES

1 **package active dry yeast**
2 **cups warm water (90°–105° F.)**
1 **cup buckwheat flour**
1 **cup unbleached white flour**
1 **teaspoon salt**
1 **tablespoon melted butter**
¼ **teaspoon baking soda**
2 **tablespoons honey or molasses**

The night before you intend to serve the pancakes, dissolve the yeast in the warm water and work in the buckwheat flour, white flour, and salt. Beat well. Cover and place the mixture in a warm place until morning. When ready to bake, add the melted butter, soda, honey or molasses, and if needed, a little extra water to thin out the batter. Bake on a lightly greased medium-hot griddle, turning once after bubbles begin to form on the unbaked side.

MAKES 4–6 SERVINGS

BUCKWHEAT BREAD WITH WHOLE WHEAT

1 **package active dry yeast**
¼ **cup warm water (90°–105° F.)**
1 **tablespoon honey**
2 **cups warm water**
3 **tablespoons oil**
6 **tablespoons honey**
2 **teaspoons salt**
4 **cups whole wheat flour**
½ **cup nonfat powdered milk**
1 **cup buckwheat flour**

The flavor of this bread is unusual and pleasing; try it even if you are not fond of buckwheat in other ways.

Dissolve the yeast in the ¼ cup water with the tablespoon honey. Allow to stand until frothy, then add the rest of the water, oil, and honey. Stir in the salt. Add the whole wheat flour, about a cupful at a time, beating with a wooden spoon. Keep beating until the batter comes away from the side of the bowl in long strings and is shiny and elastic. This happens faster if you allow the batter to stand for about ten minutes after the initial mixing. Beat in the milk powder and buckwheat flour and continue beating until all the ingredients are thoroughly combined. This sounds like a lot of beating, but since you don't knead this bread, you're still ahead in time.

Spread the batter into two well-greased baking pans, 9 × 5-inch or even a little smaller. This batter will not rise as much as some doughs made predominately from white flour and if you use too big a pan, the loaves will come out flat.

Cover the pans and allow to stand in a warm place about an hour, or until the loaves have nearly doubled in bulk.

Bake at 400° F. for forty-five minutes. Buckwheat burns easily, so if the top of the loaves seems to be getting too dark, near the end of the baking time, lay a piece of aluminum foil loosely across the top.

Cool the bread uncovered on wire racks for the crunchiest crust.

This bread is delicious served with a spread of cream cheese and chopped dates.

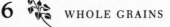

BUCKWHEAT PRETZELS

1   package active dry
     yeast
1   teaspoon sugar
1¼   cups warm water
     (90°–105° F.)
2½   cups unbleached
     white flour
½   cup buckwheat flour
1½   cups (approximately)
     unbleached white
     flour
1   egg
2   tablespoons cold
     water
Coarse salt

These pretzels passed the toughest taste test you can devise—the teenage approval test. The batch makes between eight and twelve pretzels, depending on how large you make them. Two teenage girls can finish them off before the pretzels have had a chance to cool.

Dissolve the yeast and sugar in the warm water and allow the mixture to stand until it begins to bubble—about twenty minutes. Beat in the 2½ cups unbleached white flour and continue beating until the batter becomes stretchy and shiny. Then beat in the buckwheat flour. When well mixed, knead in as much white flour as it takes to make a dough you can handle. Cover it with a damp cloth for fifteen minutes, then knead the dough until it is smooth and elastic. Place the kneaded dough in a greased bowl, cover with a damp cloth, and allow to stand until doubled in bulk. Knead down the dough and cut it into ten equal pieces. Cover the pieces and allow to rest about ten minutes, to make them easier to handle, then roll each piece into a long rope. Shape each into a pretzel form on a lightly greased cookie sheet.

Beat together the egg and cold water and use it to brush each pretzel before rising. Sprinkle coarse salt onto the moist egg wash. Kosher salt works well, as does "margarita salt" sold in the gourmet sections of some supermarkets. The egg wash makes the salt stick to the pretzels. Allow the pretzels to rise again until double in bulk. In a warm room this will take about as long as it takes to preheat the oven to 475° F. Bake about ten minutes, or until the pretzels are lightly brown but still tender.

Buckwheat pretzels are best served slightly warm and they taste especially good with a squirt of mild mustard.

MAKES 10 PRETZELS

Glen Millward photo

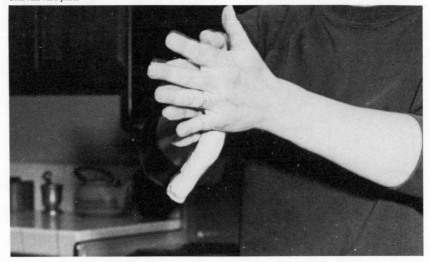

*To make pretzels,
roll dough into a rope.*

Form pretzels on cookie sheet.

Brush with egg and water.

Sprinkle with salt, let rise, bake.

They're ready in ten minutes.

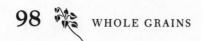

BUCKWHEAT GROATS I

½ cup buckwheat groats
2 tablespoons butter, chicken fat, or unrefined oil
1⅓ cups water

This is the simplest, basic method for cooking groats or kasha. Use this method when you are going to add the groats to other ingredients in a recipe.

Sauté the grain over medium high heat in the hot fat. Choose the fat you use according to how you'll be serving the kasha because each will lend a different flavor to the finished dish. Stir the grain constantly until you can see it begin to brown. Place your face close to the pan and sniff if you want to enjoy a delightful aroma of toasting buckwheat. But don't get so carried away with enjoying the smell that you overbrown the buckwheat—it's terrible when it burns.

As soon as the grains are browned, pour in the water, bring to a boil, lower heat, and cover the pan. Simmer for fifteen minutes, removing the pan lid for the last few minutes to evaporate any remaining moisture. This keeps the groats from turning sticky.

MAKES 4 SERVINGS

BUCKWHEAT GROATS II

1 tablespoon oil
1½ cups buckwheat groats
1 egg, beaten
2½ cups boiling water
1 teaspoon salt

This is the traditional method for cooking groats.

Use just enough of the oil to skim a fine layer on the bottom of the pan. Mix the groats and egg in the pan over low heat until the grains are all separate and coated with egg. Add the water and salt, cover, and simmer over low heat for fifteen minutes. If all the water has not been absorbed, remove the lid the last few minutes.

MAKES 6–8 SERVINGS

GROATS PILAF

2   tablespoons butter or oil
½   cup buckwheat groats
¼   cup chopped celery
¼   cup chopped onion
2   tablespoons chopped green pepper
1⅓   cup hot chicken stock
1 to 2 tablespoons soy sauce

Heat the oil over high heat in a large skillet. Stir in the groats and continue stirring rapidly until they begin to brown a little. Add the celery, onion, and green pepper and keep stirring until all the vegetables are soft. Lower the heat a little, if necessary, to avoid burning. Add the hot stock, reduce heat, cover the pan, and simmer fifteen minutes. If all the moisture has not been absorbed, finish the cooking with the lid off. Season with soy sauce to taste. Groats prepared this way are good with vegetables sautéed Chinese sytle.

MAKES 4 SERVINGS

ZUCCHINI AND GROATS CASSEROLE

2 tablespoons olive oil
1 clove garlic, minced
1 large onion, sliced
1 medium zucchini
4 cups stewed tomatoes (canned or fresh)
1 to 2 cups cooked groats prepared to recipe I.
Grated cheddar cheese

Heat the olive oil in a large skillet and add the garlic, onion, and zucchini. Stir and cook over moderately high heat until the vegetables are softened but not brown. Add the tomatoes, cover the pan, reduce heat, and cook for about ten minutes, or until squash is soft but not mushy. Plenty of liquid should remain in pan; if not, add a little water or tomato juice. Stir in the cooked groats, bring everything to a simmer, and turn into a baking dish. Top with a handful of grated cheddar cheese. Turn into a hot oven just long enough to melt cheese, and serve at once.

MAKES 6 SERVINGS

Foxtail millet (Setaria italica)

Millet

In the United States, birds probably eat more millet than people do. If you've never seen millet and wonder what it looks like, check the packages of commercial bird feed in your grocery store. The little round grains, usually ivory or yellow colored, which look like hard fish roe, are millet.

Some people call millet "poor man's cereal" because, historically, almost everyone who could eat anything else, has. Even in countries where millet has been a staple, farmers have switched to wheat and corn when it was practical. Nevertheless, millet is still a staple in many parts of the Orient and India.

It deserves a better reputation than it has because millet is nutritious; it provides good quality protein, calcium, and lecithin. It will grow on poor soil in hot, dry conditions and matures quickly.

Probably millet has not attracted more attention where growing conditions are favorable for other grains because of its bland taste. It's as mild as buckwheat is strong. For the homesteader, millet can be a substitute for rice and can provide forage and feed for animals as well.

Growing Millet

When you hear that millet comprises five genera in the tribe *Paniceae* and one genus in the tribe *Chlorideae*, and that there are a host of cultivated species in each tribe, you may decide the whole thing sounds too much like an Indian council and go back to bed. But the varieties that are actually grown in the United States and available as seeds are a manageable number and, as usual, you can rely on your seed company or Extension agent to recommend varieties suitable for your area. The reason for mentioning Latin names at all is that with millet, more than with most grains, the common names mean different things to different people. So, if you can figure out what you want under its Latin botanical name, you don't have to pronounce it, you can write it down and point — and you'll be sure of getting what you want.

Proso millet (*Panicum miliaceum*), sometimes called hog millet, is commonly grown in the North for its grain. Foxtail millet (*Setaria italica*) is usually grown in the North and the South for quick forage. And pearl millet (*Pennisetum glaucum* or *P. typhoideum*), sometimes called cattail millet, is a good choice for homesteaders and gardeners in the South because the grain easily threshes free of the hull. It is commonly grown for pasture and silage.

Prosos grow one to four feet tall, depending on variety; foxtails grow one to six feet tall; pearls grow five to ten feet high. Keep these heights in mind when you're deciding where to plant millet because anything growing that high will shade the areas near it.

Preparing Seedbed

Prepare the seedbed as for any vegetable garden crop. Even though millet is known for growing in poor soils, it does better in good soil and re-

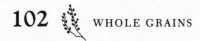
sponds to balanced fertilizer. If you are planting a solid block of millet, broadcast the seed and till or rake it in to a depth of at least one inch — more won't hurt. If you plant in rows you might try this method used in India, where manual labor still figures heavily in producing crops: the seed is dropped into furrows which have been opened with a wooden plow or hand cultivator, at the rate of about four seeds per inch. The seeds are small, so you won't be counting, but it will give you an idea of how thinly to scatter the seeds in the furrow.

In broadcasting, the seeding rate is thirty to thirty-five pounds per acre; for planting in rows, figure between six and ten pounds per acre, if you leave thirty to thirty-six inches between rows. (These figures are assuming you plant pearl millet; they would be about the same for proso, but you could use a little less foxtail, because the seed is smaller.) Depending on conditions, yield can range all the way from fifteen to sixty bushels an acre. If your millet requirements are more modest, figure on one pound for broadcasting on 1,000 square feet, and expect to harvest fifty-five pounds, more than enough for your cooking needs. Your hens (or your favorite wild birds) will love this grain and you don't have to remove the hulls for them. Millet is ready to harvest sixty to seventy-five days after seeding, depending on the variety.

Harvesting

To harvest, cut the stalks with a sickle or scythe when the seeds in the upper part of the heads are ripe and the plants are still green. The heads do not ripen uniformly — the tips may be dry and shattered before all the lower seeds are mature. Bundle the stalks in small shocks so that the green straw can dry rapidly, and if you have space, take the shocks under cover and spread them out to dry; otherwise you will lose much grain to birds and shattering.

If you thresh out the grain by banging the bundles against the inside of a large barrel, you should not damage the seed; it separates easily from the straw. Be careful about threshing with a flail or otherwise beating the millet because the seeds of some varieties crack easily. If you're using only a small amount of millet, you can remove the hulls by rubbing them off between your hands, one handful at a time.

Store millet as you would wheat or barley, the whole grain in airtight metal cans. Winnow, either before storage (this is better) or before using, by pouring the grain from one container to another in a brisk wind or before an electric fan.

Buying Millet

You can buy enough millet to make many meals for about a dollar. It's sold in natural-food stores and often in supermarkets as well. You may find a little variety in the size and color of the grains, but beyond that it's all about the same. Millet flour is available too, but is harder to find and sometimes you have to ask your natural-food store to order it. Of course, if you have a home flour mill, you can grind millet, your own or purchased, in it and have fresher flour.

Using Millet

Because of its bland taste, millet is tremendously versatile. You can substitute it in almost any recipe calling for rice, and use it in some unique ways as well. Most recipes begin with a basic cooked millet — the extra ingredients are added later.

BASIC COOKED MILLET

1 tablespoon butter
1 cup millet
3 cups water

Melt the butter and skim it across the bottom of a deep saucepan. Pour in the millet grains and, over medium high heat, stir until each grain has been coated with fat. Stir a minute or two longer to cook the starch on the outside, but do not let the grains brown more than a little. Pour in the water, bring to a boil, cover the pan, reduce the heat, and simmer for forty-five minutes, or until the grains have burst open and are tender. During the last five or ten minutes of cooking, remove the lid to evaporate any extra moisture and fluff the grains. *Do not stir* more than once, and then use a fork rather than a spoon, to avoid making the millet gooey.

No salt is included in the basic recipe because with many vegetable recipes you don't need extra salt, but you can add ½ teaspoon salt to the cooking water if you wish.

MAKES 3½ CUPS

SKILLET MILLET

¼ cup butter
1 large onion, chopped coarsely
3 to 4 cups basic cooked millet, cooled or leftover

This recipe produces a dish that is tasty and good to serve with almost anything. If more people tasted millet prepared this way, it would be more popular than it is.

A large iron skillet is the ideal utensil for this. Over medium heat melt the butter and sauté the onion until it is soft and just barely beginning to brown along the edges. Add the cooled, cooked millet and mix it well with the onion and butter. (Please use real butter — margarine is not a successful substitute.) Lower the heat to the point where the millet is just cooking. Continue cooking at this heat, stirring with a fork once or twice, for at least fifteen minutes. *Do not cover the pan.* When ready to serve, the onions should have browned somewhat more and the millet should have taken on a rich golden color. If you must, shake a little salt in the skillet before serving the millet, but taste it first because the salt in the butter may be all you need. Too much salt masks the perfect blend of brown onion, butter, and grain.

Broiled pork chops must have been invented to serve with millet prepared this way.

MAKES 4–6 SERVINGS

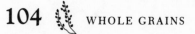

MILLET-CHARD CUSTARD

1   bunch fresh chard
    (enough to make about
    1 cup cooked)
2   tablespoons water
1   large onion, chopped
1   tablespoon butter
1   cup cooked millet
2   eggs, beaten
¼   cup milk
½   teaspoon salt

Chop the chard coarsely and cook it in the water until it is just tender. Little moisture should remain. Chop the onion and sauté it in the butter. Mix together the cooked chard, from which you've squeezed the extra moisture, onion, cooked millet, eggs, milk, and salt. Pour into a greased four-cup baking dish and bake at 350° F. for thirty minutes, or until the custard is just set.

Don't hesitate to experiment with this recipe. Try spinach instead of chard, increase the number of eggs and the amount of milk, add extra seasonings, or top with wheat germ. There's almost no way you can spoil a recipe like this.

MAKES 4 SERVINGS

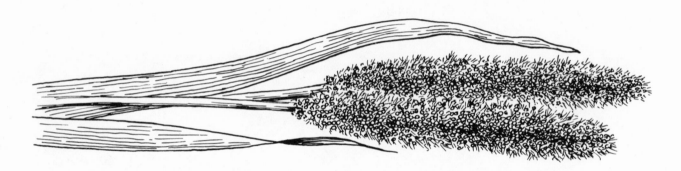

MILLET-BROCCOLI SOUFFLÉ

1   large onion, chopped
1   tablespoon butter
¼   cup butter
¼   cup flour
1   cup milk
4   eggs, separated
1   cup cooked and
    chopped broccoli
1   cup cooked millet
1   teaspoon salt

Sauté the chopped onion in the tablespoon butter until tender, and set aside. Melt the ¼ cup of butter, stir in the flour, and cook over low heat until the mixture becomes light brown. Gradually stir in the milk, beating with a whisk, to make a thick cream sauce. Cook, stirring constantly, over low to medium heat, until the sauce is very thick, then add a little of the sauce to the beaten egg yolks and mix them back into the sauce in the pan.

Beat the egg whites, which should be at room temperature, until they are stiff but not dry.

Combine the broccoli and the sautéed onion, being sure to drain off any water that may have stayed in the broccoli pan. Mix in the millet, then the cream sauce. Combine these ingredients thoroughly. Season with salt. Finally, fold in the stiffly beaten egg whites gently. Do not over-mix. Pour this mixture into a six-cup, ungreased baking dish and bake at 350° F. for forty to fifty minutes, or until the soufflé is set. Serve at once.

MAKES 6 SERVINGS

CHINESE STYLE MILLET

1   large sweet red pepper
1   large green bell pepper
1   large sweet onion
2   tablespoons oil
1   cup chicken stock
1   tablespoon cornstarch
¼   cup cold water
1   tablespoon soy sauce
3   cups cooked millet

Clean the peppers, seed them, and cut them into lengthwise slices about ¼ inch thick. Peel the onion and slice it into thin rounds.

Heat the oil in a large skillet or wok until hot but not smoking. Add the peppers and onion and stir rapidly over high heat until the vegetables begin to soften. Immediately pour in the chicken stock and bring to a boil. Stir in the cornstarch, which has been softened in the cold water, and soy sauce, lower heat and continue cooking and stirring just until the broth is thickened and has cleared. Serve over the cooked millet.

MAKES 4–6 SERVINGS

Glen Millward photo

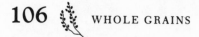

MILLET PUDDING

4 cups milk
⅓ cup maple syrup
⅓ cup millet
⅓ cup raisins
1 teaspoon vanilla
¼ cup soft bread or cake crumbs (optional)

Mix together the milk, maple syrup, millet, and raisins in a six-cup baking dish. Bake uncovered at 250° F., stirring occasionally until the pudding is thickened and the millet is tender. This will take about three hours. During the baking a brown skin will form on top of the pudding. Mix it back in each time you stir. When the pudding seems nearly thick enough, remove it from the oven and stir in the vanilla. If it seems a little curdled, which can happen when you heat milk for a long time, stir in the bread or cake crumbs and return to the oven briefly. Serve warm.

MAKES 6 SERVINGS

MINCEMEAT-MILLET PUDDING

4 cups milk
⅓ cup brown sugar
⅓ cup millet
2 cups canned mincemeat or prepared dried mincemeat
1 teaspoon vanilla

Mix the milk, sugar, and millet in a six-cup baking dish and bake, uncovered, in a 250° F. oven for three hours or until the pudding seems thick and the millet is tender. Stir from time to time during the baking. When the pudding is thick, but not as thick as you want the finished product to be, remove it from the oven and mix in the mincemeat and the vanilla. Put the dish back into the oven and continue baking until everything is very hot and you have a pleasing consistency—about twenty to thirty minutes longer. This is spectacular served hot, with a little cold, thick cream poured on it. If your oven gets too hot, you may notice some separation of the milk, but it won't change the taste at all, and the mincement more or less hides it.

MAKES 8 SERVINGS

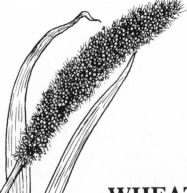

WHEAT-MILLET BREAD

2 tablespoons (packages) active dry yeast

½ cup warm water (90°–105° F.)

2 teaspoons sugar

4 cups scalded milk

¼ cup honey

1 tablespoon salt

2 tablespoons butter

12 to 13 cups unbleached white flour

¾ cup millet flour

This makes a light-textured, pale loaf, good for people who don't like 100 percent whole wheat or other heavy breads.

Soften the yeast in the warm water. Add the sugar to start the yeast growing and allow the mixture to stand for fifteen minutes. Meanwhile, scald the milk, add to it the honey, salt, and butter and cool to lukewarm. When the milk is lukewarm, add it to the yeast mixture and stir in about half the flour. Beat until the mixture is smooth and shiny and makes long strings around the bowl, then beat in the millet flour.

Finally, work in as much more unbleached white flour as it takes to make a dough you can handle. Cover the dough with a cloth and allow it to stand for fifteen minutes before you start kneading. This makes kneading much easier.

Knead the dough until you have a smooth, springy ball. Place in a lightly greased bowl, turn once to grease the surface of the dough, and cover with a damp towel. Set to rise in a warm place.

When the dough has doubled in bulk, knead it down and allow it to rise again. (It is easy to tell when your dough has doubled if you start it in a bowl that it half-fills. When the dough rises to the top of the bowl you know it's doubled.) After the second rising, shape the dough into loaves that fill the greased pans by about half. Allow to rise again until double. Bake in a 400° F. oven for thirty-five minutes.

This recipe makes four loaves if you use 8 × 5 × 2¾-inch pans. If your pans are different sizes you may have to increase or decrease the baking time a bit. The important thing is to have the dough fill whatever pans you use by about half. The recipe may also be doubled or halved.

MAKES 4 LOAVES

Oats

Mares eat oats.

And does eat oats.

And little lambs — but you remember the rest of that song.

The point is, except in Scotland, *people* eat comparatively few oats. Scotland's another story, though you'll have to decide how seriously to take it. The way the story goes is that in eastern Scotland, the unmarried plowmen didn't eat anything but oats and milk, except for an occasional potato. They got up to two quarts of milk a day and seventeen and a half pounds of oatmeal a week. And they were strong, healthy cusses. The moral depends on how much you like oatmeal and how you feel about being unmarried. Nobody seems to know what the married plowmen ate.

Whatever your marital status and nationality, eating oats is a good idea. Oats are easily digested, provide good quality protein, and are a source of several B vitamins, including inositol, and make good energy food for active outdoor people.

When it comes to growing oats, you may find that your chickens make out better than you do, because although oats are easy to grow, getting them into a form where people can enjoy them is difficult; the hull clings tenaciously in the grain's crease and hulls don't taste good.

A few hulless varieties (called *nuda* appropriately enough) exist, but they are susceptible to disease and are said not to yield well. However, these are the complaints of large-scale farmers and you might decide they don't matter much in experimenting with oats on the garden scale.

Even if you decide to buy your table oats, it might be worth growing some for the straw, which makes wonderful mulch and which horses and rabbits think makes wonderful food as well as bedding. If you've ever mulched with oat straw, you've already seen oats growing, for seeds in the straw inevitably sprout and unless you pull up the sprouts, they quickly grow into full-scale oat stalks. The stalks never seem to hurt the garden and they attract birds.

Something similar may have inspired some early experiments in oat breeding. Records show that in the late 1700s a man digging his potatoes in Scotland noticed some oats growing from a manure pile at the edge of the garden. He gathered the seed and planted it the following spring, a practice he continued from year to year, thus introducing the "potato oat."

Growing Oats

Like barley and wheat, oats are planted either in the spring or in the fall, depending on the locality, but fall varieties will not survive hard winters where average minimum temperatures drop below 10° F. On the other hand, oats are a cool weather crop and don't like searing sun, which means that if you plant spring oats you can plant them as early as the ground can be worked, and if you plant in the fall you should

109

do it late enough to avoid very hot, dry weather. Follow the local farmers. Unlike corn and millet, oats will germinate in cold ground. (In fact, if you've used much oat straw around your property and in your sheds, you may be convinced that oats will germinate anywhere. A huge truckload of oats was once stored in the machine shed of the Pitzer barn for a winter, and grain that had fallen to the ground there germinated heavily over the next eight years, fertilized only by roaming cats.)

The reputation of oats for producing a pretty good crop almost anywhere has been truly earned; good conditions produce a splendid crop.

Oats like a loamy rather than sandy soil, with a seedbed prepared well ahead of planting. Oats grow best in a soil with high nitrogen content, but this does not mean you should dump on extra nitrogen because then you'll end up with more stalk than grain. As with most garden crops, your goal should be simply a rich, naturally fertile soil, kept in that condition through good gardening practices.

Although oats usually are sown in patches, weeds are a problem this way because oats do not overpower them as does buckwheat, and because there's no good way to get into a solid patch to pull out the most aggressive weeds. There's no good reason why you couldn't plant your oats in broad bands or rows, a foot or so wide, with enough space between rows for you and your cultivator, hoe, or tiller. You don't have to cultivate within the row, but just keeping the spaces between rows clean will cut down considerably on choking weeds.

Sowing

Work the seedbed or rows until fine but not powdery, broadcast the seed at the rate of about 2½ bushes per acre, or less if you plant in rows. Rake or till in the seed to a depth of one to two inches. If you're dealing with a small length of row, it would help to lay a plank over the row, after working in the seed, and walk it to increase the contact between soil and seed. For 1000 square feet, sow two pounds of oats and expect to harvest about fifty pounds.

During the early part of the growing season, pull out any weeds that threaten to take over, and that's it until harvest time.

Harvesting

On a small scale, harvesting with a sickle or scythe is the simplest approach, especially if you planted your oats in rows. If you're growing the oats for grain, you can use the farmer's rub and bite test to see if it's time to harvest: Rub the heads between your hands to see if the grain comes out easily and then bite on a piece of grain. If it's hard against your teeth, it's ready. If threshed grain is not your main concern, you can harvest the oats while some of the stalks are still green and the grain is in what is called the "milk" stage. Either way, you can harvest and store oats exactly as you would handle wheat. Check our lengthy description of the process in the chapter on wheat.

Some homesteaders cure cut oats like hay, raking them into rows on the ground to dry, turning them once or twice to dry the underside, and then hauling them in. You lose some of the grain this way, but probably not enough to matter on the small scale, especially since you may not be using your home-grown oats for the table.

Commercial growers hull the oats with elaborate machinery and make rolled oats by heating the grain and flattening it with rollers and steam. The problem with home-improvised hulling is that you just can't get rid of enough of the hull to make the oats or oat flour palatable and oats don't grind well in a home mill because they're too soft. Even farmers with graineries full buy their oatmeal in the grocery store.

Buying Oats

You can buy oats easily in any of seven ways: whole with hulls, whole hulled (groats), steel cut, rolled (regular, quick, and instant), and flour.

Whole oats, with the hulls still on them, are sold in seed stores and sometimes by farmers.

Oat groats, with hulls removed, are found in natural-food stores. Two methods are used to remove the hulls commercially. One is to heat the oats and, when they are dry, run them through hulling stones to break off the brittle hulls. The

Harvesting oats in Minnesota many years ago.

Oat field near Mission Range, Minnesota.

other method is to use a huller, a device that slams the grains against a surface, cracking the hulls, which then can be winnowed out.

Steel-cut oats, groats that have been sliced into pieces with steel blades, are sold in natural-food stores and, occasionally, in natural-food sections of supermarkets.

Rolled oats, groats that have been steamed and run through rollers to flatten them, are sold in all kinds of food stores. Quaker Oats is probably the most famous brand. This is what people think of when you talk about oatmeal.

Quick-cooking rolled oats are thinner than regular rolled oats because the groats have been cut into pieces before rolling. Supermarkets and natural-food stores sell them.

Instant rolled oats are made from partly cooked groats pieces and rolled even thinner than quick oats. These are rarely sold in natural-food stores because they're considered over-processed, but they fill the shelves in super-markets. They are too expensive to be a good buy.

Oat flour, or ground groats, is sold in natural-food stores. It contains all of the oat but the hull. Usually you can buy it in bulk so you need take only as much as you can use in a short time.

Although a good natural-food store is the best place to find oats in all these forms, there's absolutely nothing wrong with supermarket oats. Do not make the mistake of assuming that oats you buy in natural-food stores are organically grown. Only if they are specifically so labeled can you count on that.

Using Oats

Oats are interesting to cook with because they can be prepared in so many different ways, each with its own special taste. Of course out of respect for those Scottish plowmen and for every grandmother who ever cooked up a pot of oatmeal, we have to start with oatmeal. All the recipes included here are for steel-cut or regular rolled oats, not the quick-cook kinds.

BASIC OATMEAL

4 cups water
¼ teaspoon salt
2 cups rolled oats

Bring the water to a rolling boil, add salt, stir in oats, and lower heat. Cook about five minutes, but do not stir more than once or twice. Remove the pan from the heat, cover it, and allow to stand for as long as twenty minutes before serving. The longer it stands the more creamy the oatmeal will be. If you like it to be very creamy, start the oats in cold water; if you like a coarser texture, shorten the cooking and standing times.

MAKES 6–8 SERVINGS

DOUBLE-BOILER OATMEAL

2 cups water
¼ teaspoon salt
1 cup rolled oats

The old *Settlement Cookbook* says the double-boiler method produces a better flavor. That's debatable, but it certainly does take longer.

Bring the water to a boil in the top of a double boiler, stir in the salt and the oats and cook over direct heat for five minutes, stirring constantly. Meanwhile bring water to a boil in the bottom half of the double boiler, and at the end of the five minutes, place the oatmeal in the double boiler top over the bottom half and cover. Steam over low heat for thirty minutes or longer.

MAKES 4 SERVINGS

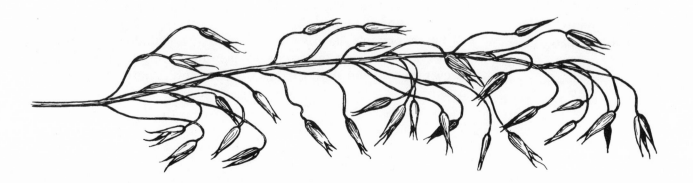

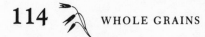

STEEL-CUT OATMEAL

1 cup steel-cut oats
4 cups water
¼ teaspoon salt

Mix all ingredients and allow to stand overnight in the refrigerator. Next morning bring to a boil, lower heat, and cover pan. Cook gently until the moisture is absorbed and the oats are tender, usually about one hour, depending on the dryness of the oats when you started. This oatmeal has a texture different from that made with rolled oats.

MAKES 4 SERVINGS

STEEL-CUT OATMEAL, ONE-HOUR METHOD

1 cup steel-cut oats
3 cups cold water
½ teaspoon salt

Bring water to a boil in bottom of a double boiler, and turn heat to medium. Put all ingredients in top of double boiler, cover, and cook for one hour. Do not overcook. Does not need to be stirred. Can be reheated.

MAKES 3–4 SERVINGS

TEXTURED OATMEAL

1 cup rolled oats
1½ cups boiling water
¼ teaspoon salt

This is for people who don't like creamy oatmeal and prefer some coarseness to remain.

Put the oats in a warm baking dish with a tight lid. Pour the boiling water and salt over them and stir just until everything is mixed. Cover the dish and allow to stand for about five minutes before serving.

MAKES 4 SERVINGS

Tall oats. Photo taken in 1915.

FRIED OATMEAL

A woman who grew up in Alaska says this was her family's standard breakfast and it warded off the chill for a long morning. The addition of the fat it is fried in and the syrup or honey it is served with probably helped.

Prepare cooked oatmeal according to any of the preceding recipes or use leftover. If you cook oatmeal especially for this recipe, use a little less water for the same effect of thickening you get when oatmeal sits around after being left over.

Pour the cooked oatmeal into a buttered loaf pan and refrigerate at least twenty-four hours. Slice as needed, dust lightly with flour, and

Glen Millward photo

To fry oatmeal, cut in slices.

Dust slices with flour.

fry over moderately high heat in a little butter. Serve hot with maple syrup, honey, or molasses.

If you're tempted to skip dusting the oatmeal slices with flour, you should know that it makes the fried slices crisper on the outside.

You could increase the nutritive value of fried oatmeal by stirring in a handful of wheat germ or a small amount of non-instant powdered milk before pouring the oatmeal into a loaf pan for chilling. You'll have to fry the slices more cautiously then, because both milk powder and wheat germ burn easily on high heat.

To jazz up the flavor of fried oatmeal, you could stir in some maple syrup or dark molasses or cinnamon and raisins before turning it into the pan to chill.

Glen Millward photo

Fry in a little butter.

Serve hot with maple syrup or honey.

GRANOLA

7	cups rolled oats
1	cup rolled wheat flakes
1	cup triticale flakes
¼	cup non-instant powdered milk

1	cup wheat germ
1	cup ground sesame seeds
1	cup raw sunflower seeds
1	cup raw peanuts

1	cup raisins or dried apple bits
½	cup oil
½	cup honey
1	tablespoon vanilla

I suppose there must be a thousand recipes for granola. This is a Pitzer favorite and is offered here mainly to suggest a base for your improvisation.

Mix together the first four ingredients in a large, flat pan. Bake in a preheated 400° F. oven for about five minutes, stirring several times. Remove from the oven and add the wheat germ, sesame seeds, hulled sunflower seeds, and peanuts. Toast about five minutes more, stirring often. Remove from the oven. Mix together the raisins, oil, honey, and vanilla. Pour this over the granola mixture and stir thoroughly until all the flakes are coated. Return to the oven and toast again, for about two minutes, or just long enough to bake in the honey.

Remove from the oven and cool very thoroughly before storing in a large jar or can.

MAKES ABOUT 14 CUPS

LIGHT OATMEAL BREAD

2 cups boiling water
1½ cups rolled oats
2 teaspoons salt
¼ cup honey
1 package active dry yeast
¼ cup warm water (90°–105° F.)
1 teaspoon sugar
¼ cup wheat germ
About 5 cups unbleached white flour

The texture of this bread is just slightly coarser than white bread, but its extra moisture compensates. It makes wonderful sandwiches.

Pour the boiling water over the rolled oats in a large bowl. Add the salt and honey and cool to lukewarm. Dissolve the yeast with the teaspoon of sugar in the ¼ cup warm water. When the yeast mixture is bubbling, add it to the cooled oatmeal mixture, then beat in the wheat germ and about half the flour. When the mixture is shiny and elastic, work in as much more flour as you need to make a dough you can handle. Knead until the dough is smooth and springy. Allow to rise until double in bulk, knead down, and shape into loaves. Allow to rise in greased 8 × 5-inch pans until double again. Bake at 375° F. about fifty minutes. This recipe may be doubled or divided.

MAKES 2 LOAVES

STEEL-CUT OAT BREAD

1 cup steel-cut oats
¼ cup dark molasses
1 tablespoon butter
½ teaspoon salt
2 cups boiling water
1 package active dry yeast
¼ cup warm water (90°–105° F.)
1 teaspoon sugar
¼ cup wheat germ
2 cups unbleached white flour

Like the previous recipe, this one makes a coarser-textured bread; it has such a good taste it wouldn't even need butter.

Mix the oats, molasses, butter, and salt in a large bowl. Pour in the boiling water and allow the mixture to stand until it has reached room temperature.

Dissolve the yeast in the warm water with the sugar and allow to stand until frothy. Pour the yeast mixture into the cooled oat mixture and then stir in the wheat germ and unbleached flour. Use enough flour to make a dough you can handle. This could be a little more or less than two cups.

Turn the dough onto a floured surface, form it into a ball, cover it with a damp cloth, and allow it to stand for fifteen minutes. Next, knead until the dough is very springy and elastic. The standing period makes the kneading easier and faster.

Put the dough into a greased mixing bowl, cover with a damp cloth, and allow it to rise in a warm place until double in bulk.

Punch down the dough and shape into one large loaf (about 5 × 9 inches) or two "miniature" loaves. Allow to stand, again covered with a damp cloth, until double in bulk.

Bake about forty minutes at 375° F. Shorten the baking time if you make two smaller loaves.

MAKES 1 OR 2 LOAVES

WHEAT-OAT BREAD

1 **package active dry yeast**

¼ **cup warm water (90°–105° F.)**

1 **teaspoon sugar**

2 **cups warm water**

1 **teaspoon salt**

3 **tablespoons oil**

¼ **cup honey**

4 **cups whole wheat flour**

½ **cup unbleached white flour**

½ **cup oat flour (or rolled oats ground in your blender)**

¼ **cup nonfat powdered milk**

This bread is delicious, one of the best ever, and so easy it's almost embarrassing. It's especially good with cheese and, if you're careful not to burn the edges, makes marvelous toast. With a little peanut butter, it's nearly a meal.

Dissolve the yeast in the ¼ cup warm water and stir in the sugar. Allow the mixture to stand until it is frothy. Mix it in a large bowl with two cups warm water, salt, oil, and honey. Gradually beat in about three cups of the whole wheat flour. Continue beating until the mixture is shiny and elastic and pulls away from the sides of the bowl in long strings, then beat in the white flour, the oat flour, and the powdered milk. Beat very well, until all the ingredients are thoroughly combined. At this point you really can't overbeat. Finally, beat in as much more of the whole wheat flour as you need to make a stiff batter. You will not be kneading it, so you don't have to make a dough you can handle, just one that will stand up fairly well in the pans.

Turn the batter into well-greased pans about 5 × 9 inches or a little smaller. If the pans are too big, the loaves will be flat. The batter should at least half-fill them.

Allow the pans to stand in a warm place, covered by a damp cloth, until the batter comes to the top of the pans or is about doubled in bulk.

Bake in a preheated 400° F. oven for forty-five minutes.

MAKES 2 LOAVES

OATMEAL MUFFINS

1 cup rolled oats
1 cup buttermilk
1 egg
½ cup honey
1 cup flour
½ teaspoon salt
1 teaspoon baking
   powder
½ teaspoon baking soda
¼ cup melted butter

Soak the oats in the buttermilk for two hours, then add the egg and beat well. Stir in the honey. Sift together the dry ingredients and stir them in. Finally, mix in the melted butter. Bake in greased muffin pans in a 400° F. oven for fifteen to twenty minutes.

MAKES 1 DOZEN MUFFINS

Grant Heilman Photography

OATMEAL COOKIES

¾ cup vegetable shortening

1 cup firmly packed brown sugar

½ cup granulated sugar

1 egg

¼ cup water

1 teaspoon vanilla

3 cups rolled oats

1 cup unbleached white flour

1 teaspoon salt

½ teaspoon soda

Some things in this world are such traditions and are so fine as they are that they should not be changed. This old favorite from Quaker Oats is a case in point, although you can cut down a little on the sugar if you wish.

Cream together the shortening and sugars until creamy; beat in the egg, water, and vanilla and mix very well. Combine the dry ingredients and stir them into the sugar-shortening mixture. Drop by rounded teaspoonsful onto a greased cookie sheet and bake in a 350° F. preheated oven for twelve to fifteen minutes. Cool completely on racks before storing.

MAKES ABOUT 5 DOZEN COOKIES

OATMEAL-PEANUT COOKIES

¾ cup firmly packed brown sugar

½ cup granulated sugar

¼ cup peanut butter

½ cup vegetable shortening

1 egg

¼ cup water

1 teaspoon vanilla

3 cups rolled oats

1 cup unbleached white flour

1 teaspoon salt

½ teaspoon soda

1 cup raw peanuts

Cream together the sugars, shortening, and peanut butter until creamy. Beat in the egg, water, and vanilla and mix very well. Combine the dry ingredients and stir them into the sugar-shortening mixture. Work in the raw peanuts, being sure they are evenly distributed. Drop batter by rounded teaspoonsful onto a greased cookie sheet and bake in a 350° F. preheated oven twelve to fifteen minutes. Cool completely on racks before storing.

MAKES ABOUT 5½ DOZEN COOKIES

Oatmeal cookies.

CRACKED OAT PATTIES

½ cup steel-cut oats
2 tablespoons butter
2 cups water or stock
Salt
Chopped parsley
Gravy

Oats seem to lend themselves to baked goods more than to main dish kinds of cooking, but the following recipe makes a substitute for potatoes or noodles.

Sauté the oats in the butter until each grain is well coated, then pour in the stock, cover the pan tightly, and lower heat to simmer. Simmer, without stirring, for about an hour. If the heat is low and the lid is tight, the oats will not burn or stick seriously to the bottom of the pan. Stirring makes them gooey. At the end of the hour, remove the lid and continue cooking, if necessary, to evaporate excess moisture. Let the mixture cool. (Incidentally, this recipe is good just like it is at this stage, eaten with a spoon.)

Shape the cooled oats into six small patties and chill them overnight or for several hours. When ready to serve, brown the patties, first on one side, then the other, sprinkling lightly with salt and chopped parsley. Serve with gravy.

MAKES 3 SERVINGS

SCOTTISH MINESTRONE

½ cup whole oats (not cracked or rolled)

2 cups water

½ head cabbage

3 stalks celery

1 medium onion

1 clove garlic

2 tablespoons olive oil

¼ cup chopped parsley

4 cups cooked or canned tomatoes

4 cups mixed vegetables, fresh or frozen (green beans, corn, limas, turnip, etc.)

1 cup cooked beans (navy, garbanzo, pink, or any combinations)

Water or stock

Pinch of salt if necessary

Now there's a name that ought to confuse the Italians and the Scots alike. Laugh all you want, but the combination of oats and beans makes this a protein-rich soup.

Put the oats and water into a small pan, bring to a boil, cover, lower heat to simmer, and cook for about an hour, or until the grains have burst open and are tender but still chewy.

Chop the cabbage, celery, and onion. Mince the garlic.

In the soup kettle heat the olive oil and sauté the garlic and parsley in it until the garlic begins to soften. Toss in the chopped vegetables and stir them in the oil and garlic. As soon as they are somewhat coated with the oil, add the tomatoes, cover the pot, and simmer until the celery is tender.

Add the cooked oats, the mixed vegetables, and the cooked beans, along with enough water or stock (you could use some of the bean liquid and any liquid left from the oats) to achieve the level of soupiness you prefer. Bring to a gentle simmer and cook everything just until the mixed vegetables are done. Do not overcook.

Serve this soup with grated cheese and buckwheat pretzels (see p. 96) and everyone will go away groaning in delight.

MAKES 10–12 SERVINGS

Rice

As you learn how complicated it is to grow rice, you may marvel that it's the principal food crop of about half the world's population. In the United States, rice is grown commercially in parts of California, Texas, Louisiana, Arkansas, Mississippi, Missouri, South Carolina, and Florida. Rice requires wet soil and a growing season four to six months long with a mean temperature of at least 70° F. Although most varieties, known as *paddy rice*, need to be grown where the crop can be flooded, some, known as *upland rice*, will grow without flooding if the soil can be kept wet. Deep-water rice, which has culms that float on top of the water, grows in areas where deep, rapid flooding happens naturally. American texts say floating rice is harvested by hand from boats, but some photographs in Asian texts show workers up to their necks in water, harvesting the rice. All this gives you some idea how demanding rice culture can be.

Unless you've mastered most other kinds of horticulture and are looking for a new challenge, you may be more interested in the section in this chapter on buying rice than in the information about how to grow it. No one associated with this book has ever tried to grow rice; the information here has been gleaned from agricultural texts aimed at commercial growers and translated as much as possible into small garden terms. A short bibliography at the end of this chapter will guide you if you want to read more about rice culture.

Growing Rice

According to a U.S. Department of Agriculture Farmer's Bulletin, you must meet the following requirements to be able to grow rice: warm temperatures during the entire growing season; abundant water for irrigation; level areas with soil that will hold water without much seepage; and good surface drainage to get rid of the water when you no longer want it, at harvest time. You probably stand the best chance of meeting these requirements if you live in one of the areas mentioned where rice is grown commercially. Otherwise, creating the necessary conditions may be a test of your ingenuity and determination.

First, you will have to decide whether you want to grow your rice in a nursery bed and transplant the young plants, as is common in many Asian countries, or seed it directly where it is to grow to maturity. In the United States, commercial growers don't transplant, but broadcast the rice, often by airplane, onto the fields where it is to grow. In California, most of the fields are submerged in water before the seeding operation to help control weeds, and the grain is soaked anywhere from twenty-four hours to almost a month (generally in circulating water) so that it won't float when broadcast and so that it will germinate faster.

Reducing all this to the garden scale, you

could choose between seeding soaked rice at the rate of about 140 pounds per acre (dry weight) where it is to grow, either before or after you submerge the plot, or geminating the seeds in a thickly sown (about 150 pounds per acre) nursery bed and then transplanting the plants. The main advantage of the first method is that you handle everything only once; the advantage of the second method is that you have to control weeds in a smaller area while the rice is germinating and in its young stages.

Preparing the Plot

Either way, you will need a sunny growing area that can be submerged, although if you have a spot with exceptionally good drainage and an unlimited water supply, you might get interesting results experimenting with constant mist instead. To prepare the seedbed, till or spade the ground either in the fall or the early spring, concentrating on getting rid of weeds and leveling the soil. If you do this in the fall, you will probably want to go over it lightly again in the spring to hit the new weed growth. How you create your paddy will depend on the topography of your land, but figure that it will be easier to flood several small areas than one large one. One approach would be to dig trenches several inches apart and block them up at each end. The Japanese used to use a technique similar to this, growing rice in the trough and barley on the ridges. It definitely will be to your advantage to plant your rice in rows rather than blocks, whether you transplant or direct seed, because you can get in to weed more easily.

Don't plant until the soil and air are in the neighborhood of 75° F., probably sometime between April 1 and June 1. Your irrigation water should be warm too, which may mean rigging up a holding tank or pond if you're using cold spring or well water. Consider also whether you can arrange a gravity-feed system, can use the pump that provides household water, or will need a separate pump.

Planting

At planting time, spread the seed thickly enough to cover the ground if you're transplanting, or more sparsely if seeding direct, onto your thoroughly prepared and smoothed seedbed. If you've worked in good organic matter during preparation, so much the better. Tramp the rice down carefully and cover it lightly with mulch or sand. Next begin gentle watering; don't flood anything yet.

In about a week, young shoots should begin to appear. When the plants are obviously up and growing, you can begin to flood the paddy. Commercial operations flood by about eight inches and keep the area continuously submerged; home operations may get by with as little as an inch of water, and some rice gardeners recommend draining the paddy each night and reflooding it each morning to discourage mosquitoes and to give the sunlight and oxygen more chance at the plants. How much of the time your rice should be flooded and how much of it should be drained depends so much on soil conditions and weather that all we can reasonably suggest is that you experiment with more or less water and try to judge how the plants are responding. Commercial operations sometimes increase the water level gradually to keep up with the plants' growth. Whatever you do, keep weeding; rice doesn't like to compete for its nutrients. Grow the plants on for about thirty-five days or until they reach a height of five to seven inches, then either thin slightly in the case of direct seeding, or transplant.

When transplanting, drain the bed and gently pull up the plants. At the same time you should be watering the area into which the plants are to be moved thoroughly enough to make mud. What you do next depends on whose advice you take. Some rice gardeners say they simply replant, others first trim the tops back by a little less than a third before transplanting. Again, you will have to experiment if this is your first try and you're planning to become an expert on

leaving yourself some sort of access to the rows for weeding. The same would be true of direct seeding, which is why some thinning might be necessary as the seedlings grow if you got over-enthusiastic in the amount of seed you planted.

If you haven't been draining the paddy every night or didn't try heavy watering instead of flooding, you should drain the paddy when the plants are about fifteen inches high, cultivate it, and then flood it again.

Harvesting

Finally, drain the water from the rice field before the crop is fully mature, when the rice is fully headed and beginning to ripen — about two weeks before maturity. This allows the grain to finish ripening and, incidentally, is going to make it a lot easier to work at harvest.

If you've never seen mature rice growing, harvest condition may be a little difficult to determine. The grain will be ready four to six months after you planted it, depending on the variety, and this information will come from your seed supplier. Basically, when rice is ready to harvest, it will look like other grain heads, brownish gold and heavy. Trust your eye. If you've been watching those plants since they were sprouts, following each stage, you will almost certainly recognize ripeness, even if you've never seen it before.

Surprisingly enough, after having gone through the rather complicated growing procedure, you harvest rice as you would wheat or any other grain in your garden. After cutting and bundling it, let it dry, either in shocks or on the ground if the weather is dry, or someplace under roof with good circulation where you can spread out the rice. If you are harvesting only an experimental row or two, you might try the old method of Indonesia, where the heads are cut off one at a time, and the straw is left in the field.

You thresh and winnow rice the same as any other grain, too.

growing rice. Trimming the plants *is* consistent with transplanting practices for many other kinds of plants, the idea being to give the roots less foliage demanding support until they become reestablished in their new soil.

In Japan the trimmed seedlings are pushed into the mud in rows about a foot apart, several seedlings to a hill, with the hills something like five inches apart in the row. Some rice is transplanted into rows without hills. There definitely are no rules on this yet for the home rice gardener in the United States except for allowing enough space for the plants to grow fully and

Removing the Hulls

The threshed and winnowed grain, with hulls intact, is known as paddy or rough rice. You can't eat it until you remove some of the tough hulls. Even the writers most lyrical about the joys of growing it yourself admit that hulling rice is pure chore. One old Asian way is to pound the grain with a wooden mallet or work it with a big wooden mortar and pestle.

Several Japanese firms make small hand rice hullers, though they are not generally available in this country. See Appendix for sources. You might improvise your own by putting together a series of hand-cranked rollers which scratch the grain across a rough surface. And on a very small scale indeed, you can experiment with something like a wooden salad bowl and an improvised pestle such as the end of a French rolling pin. After using any such method, you'd have to clean the grain again to get rid of loose hulls and dirt. Store cleaned rice as you would any other grain.

Buying Rice

Even if you have to walk five miles on a wooden leg to get to the store, buying rice is easier than growing and cleaning it. It's available in natural-food stores and supermarkets at low prices and in considerable variety. Organically grown rice is harder to find. Arrowhead Mills, Chico-San, and Lone Pine Farm brands are labeled organic. Organically grown rice will be more expensive than that grown with pesticides and chemical fertilizers because organic growers are operating on a smaller scale and haven't the benefit of the economies of a big commercial operation. One nutritionist has observed that one thing you can count on is that if rice is cheap, it's not organic.

However, if you are willing to forego the organic label, you will find you can buy a surprising variety of rice. Let's dismiss at once "instant"

THE MANY FORMS OF RICE

INSTANT RICE   Lacks both taste and nutrition. Avoid it.

POLISHED WHITE RICE   Beautiful white, at the price of much of rice's nutritional qualities. The hulls, bran, germ, and endosperm have been removed in the polishing.

CONVERTED RICE   Rice that has been soaked and steamed before milling, to retain more of the vitamins and nutrients.

BROWN RICE   Rice that has been hulled, so that much of its nutritional qualities has been retained.

WHITE RICE FLOUR   Made from polished white rice, so has little taste, low nutritional qualities.

BROWN RICE FLOUR   Faint taste, more nutritional than white rice flour.

RICE POLISHINGS   The bran and other materials milled off brown rice.

WILD RICE   Not a true rice; commonly found growing wild in the Great Lakes region. A nutritional, tasty, and expensive food product.

---

rice, which is an embarrassment to America and won't be considered here any more seriously than we would consider styrofoam white bread or plastic roses — either of which might be more palatable. And then there is polished white rice, which is sold in great quantity and gave plantation workers beriberi back in the late 1800s, until someone thought to replace in their diet the B vitamins that were being polished off the rice. Less than ten years ago, white rice was all you could find on most grocery store shelves. These days, probably because of the growing interest in nutrition, most stores that carry white rice also carry converted rice and brown rice.

Converted rice is a little better for you than white rice because it is partially cooked before milling by a soaking and steaming process which shoves some of the nutrients from the hulls into the grain so that fewer vitamins and minerals will be lost when the bran is polished away. Converted rice is more expensive than either white rice or regular brown rice, and is about the same price as organic brown rice.

Brown rice is paddy rice that has been hulled and thus lost some, but by no means all, of its bran, germ, and endosperm. Like white rice, it is available in long-grained, medium-grained, and short-grained varieties. To give you an idea of what happens when brown rice is polished to white: about 10 percent of its protein, 85 percent of its fat, and 70 percent of its minerals are removed. What's left hardly seems worth the water you boil it in. Ironically, you can go to the natural-food store and *buy* rice polishings.

In addition to deciding on white or brown rice, you have to choose among short-, medium-, and long-grain rices. Although you can use these pretty much interchangeably in recipes, you may be surprised at the differences among them in taste and texture. Generally, the short-grain rices tend to be a little more soft and moist and the grains will stick together somewhat. Long-grain rice cooks up into a dryer product, with the grains tending to remain separate. The flavor of short-grain rice is somewhat more sweet and pronounced than that of long-grain rice. Medium-grained rice, which you can't always find, tends to have the flavor of short-grained rice and the texture of the long-grained. The part of the country where you live will determine to some extent what rice you can buy. For instance, you're not apt to find Carolina rice in California or vice-versa. If, until now, you've eaten only converted, instant, and white rice, you will be surprised at how much difference in taste and texture you can enjoy as you experiment with the various grain lengths in rice from different parts of the country.

Other Rice Products

Other rice products you can buy include white and brown rice flour and rice polishings. White rice flour has about the same nutritional value as white rice and it has almost no taste. Brown rice flour is only a little darker than the white, is more nutritious, and has a faint taste. Both flours are usually sold in natural-food stores and some specialty and Oriental shops. About the only place you can buy rice polishings, which as we've said are what's milled off the brown rice, is in a natural-food store. Rice flour is commonly used by people who are allergic to wheat or have digestive problems. The polishings are used mainly by people looking for natural sources of B vitamins and add nothing to speak of in the way of good taste or texture.

Using Rice

Of all the whole grains, rice is probably the easiest to introduce to people accustomed only to refined foods. Brown rice has a pleasant but mild flavor and the grain cooks up to be just slightly chewy — not tough and not mushy. If you've had trouble cooking rice so that it doesn't turn out gummy, you'll be glad to know that brown rice almost never sticks together.

After my family had been eating brown rice for about a year, I became interested in Chinese cooking and in the interests of "authenticity," I picked up a box of converted white rice, because

---

HOW TO MAKE SESAME OIL

Toast ½ cup of sesame seeds in a heavy, ungreased skillet. Add one cup of peanut oil. Place the skillet in a 280° oven for ten minutes, to get the flavor of the seeds into the oil. Cool the mixture.

Blend the seeds and oil in a blender at high speed until it makes a paste. Let the mixture sit overnight, then filter the oil through a cloth.

I'd read that the Chinese prefer white rice. Everyone in the family commented on the fact that the rice that night seemed tasteless. The rest of the box is still on the back of a shelf somewhere. I thought I might use it to make beanbags sometime.

The recipes for rice are practically limitless.

Some of them begin with raw rice, some call for cooked rice. Following are recipes for the two basic ways of cooking rice, steamed and as pilaf. Emphatically, you *do not* need an electric rice cooker or any other exotic gadget to make good rice. A regular pan and attention to instructions suffice.

More About Growing Rice

Where to read more about growing rice:

Hunt, Thomas F. *The Cereals in America.* New York: Orange Judd Company, 1914.

Wilson, Howard K. *Grain Crops.* New York: McGraw-Hill Book Company, Inc., 1948.

Leonard, Warren H., and Martin, John H. *Cereal Crops.* New York: The Macmillan Company, 1963.

Logsdon, Gene. *Small-Scale Grain Raising.* Emmaus, Pa.: Rodale Press, Inc. 1977.

Kingman, Maryanna. *The Book of Whole Grains.* New York: St. Martin's Press, 1976.

The older books are valuable because they describe growing rice before the age of total technology; the Leonard and Martin book describes the process as it is practiced in Japan and as it has come to be practiced more recently in this country; the Logsdon and Kingman books deal, briefly, with growing rice at home.

BASIC STEAMED RICE

1 cup raw brown rice
2½ cups water
2 teaspoons butter (optional)
½ teaspoon salt (optional)

If the rice looks dusty, wash it by letting water run over it in a colander or sieve. Brown rice sometimes has a little debris left when you buy it.

Mix the rice and water in a large, flat-bottomed saucepan with a tight lid. Leave the pan uncovered while you bring the rice to a boil over high heat. As soon as the water is boiling you can add the salt and butter if you want to. Many recipes call for them, but neither is necessary and, in fact, if you tasted rice cooked with and without these two ingredients, you probably wouldn't notice the difference because brown rice, having a flavor of its own, doesn't need the boost.

As soon as the water and rice have come to a boil, cover the pan and turn the heat to low so that you are cooking at just a simmer. Allow the rice to cook this way for about forty minutes, then lift the lid to see how much liquid is left. If there's still quite a bit of moisture in the pan, leave the lid off as the rice continues to cook for five or ten minutes more. You'll probably see some recipes instructing you to cook brown rice for up to an hour. Although it won't hurt, it usually isn't necessary to cook it that long. In any case, do the final few minutes of cooking with the lid off to dry out the grains a little and eliminate unwanted starchiness.

MAKES ABOUT 3½ CUPS

BASIC PILAF

2 tablespoons butter or oil
1 cup raw brown rice
2½ cups liquid (water or stock)
½ teaspoon salt

Wash and drain the rice if necessary. Melt the butter or place the oil in a heavy skillet with a tight lid over high heat, but take care not to let the fat burn. Pour in the rice and stir it in the hot fat for a few minutes, until each grain is coated and just beginning to brown slightly. Immediately pour in the liquid and add the salt. As soon as the mixture has come to a boil, turn the heat to low, cover the pan, and simmer gently for about forty minutes. At this point, proceed as you did in the previous recipe, checking for excess moisture and cooking it off if necessary.

If you wish to add chopped onion, celery, mushrooms, parsley, or other vegetables, sauté them along with the rice before adding the liquid. And if you use a stock or broth which already contains salt, don't add any more in the cooking.

MAKES ABOUT 3½ CUPS

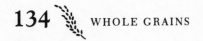

CHINESE FRIED RICE

2   tablespoons oil

2   eggs

1   cup raw sliced vege-
    tables (green pepper,
    scallions, celery, bean
    sprouts, peas, carrots,
    cabbage, etc.)

2   cups cooked (cold)
    brown rice

Soy sauce

½   cup cooked, slivered
    chicken, pork, or fish

½   cup chopped spinach
    or chard

Toasted sesame seed oil

If the only fried rice you've ever tried has been white, you're in for a wonderful surprise when you try it made with brown rice. The ingredients given here should be considered suggestions, not rules that can't be changed. Go by what you have around the house and what you like. Make extra rice and use the leftover for this.

Wipe the bottom of your iron skillet or wok with a bit of the oil, beat the eggs with a fork, and make a small, thin omelet of them. Remove from the skillet, shred, and set aside.

Put about one tablespoon more oil in the skillet and stir-fry the chopped raw vegetables briefly over high heat. Remove from the pan and set aside. Do not cook the vegetables until they are tender; they should remain crisp. Put the rest of the oil in the skillet, heat for a moment, and then add the cold rice. Stir it in the pan, over medium-high heat, breaking up any lumps and making sure all the grains come in contact with the bottom of the pan from time to time. When all the rice is hot and beginning to look a little fried, season with soy sauce, stir again, and put in the sautéed vegetables and shredded omelet. Stir together briefly, adding the chopped spinach and the slivered meat, chicken, or fish as you do. Do not try to mix everything thoroughly. You actually want to leave some of the vegetables and most of the meat on top. Sprinkle some sesame oil on top and serve immediately. (The sesame oil here is not cold-pressed salad oil, but oil made from toasted sesame seeds. You'll find it in Oriental shops, specialty stores, and the gourmet sections of supermarkets. If you don't find it, get some from a Chinese restaurant or get a natural-food store to order it for you. It's worth the trouble. No other oil is an adequate substitute for flavor.)

MAKES 4 SERVINGS

SARA'S FRIED RICE

2 tablespoons oil
2 cups cold cooked
brown rice
2 teaspoons sugar
½ teaspoon salt
¼ cup chopped scallions
or onion
¼ cup thinly sliced
celery
¼ cup pine nuts or
cashews
½ cup cooked shrimp,
chicken, pork,
or turkey
¼ cup raisins
1 just-ripe banana,
diced

This recipe is based on one from Julia Child in a vague sort of way, but Julia uses white rice rather than brown rice. (Gourmets don't like to be caught in the act of willful nutrition.)

Heat half the oil in the skillet until it is almost smoking. Add the rice and stir it rapidly, over medium high heat, until all the grains are coated with a little oil and beginning to look fried. Sprinkle the sugar and salt on top, stir a minute more, and turn the rice into a large warm serving dish. Quickly heat the rest of the oil and add the scallions, celery, and nuts. Stir for a minute, then remove the pan from the heat and stir in the shrimp, raisins, and (gently) the banana. Pour all these ingredients onto the top of the rice, after making an indentation with your spoon or spatula to hold everything.

Each diner scoops up rice and a portion of the goodies in the middle to serve himself.

Vary the ingredients according to your own taste. For instance, canned mandarin orange sections, diced apples, and bits of pineapple are good. In the vegetable line you could include red sweet pepper, water cress, or finely diced rutabaga.

MAKES 4 SERVINGS

ORANGE CASHEW RICE

3   **tablespoons butter**

⅔   **cup diced celery**

2   **tablespoons finely chopped onion**

1½   **cup water**

1   **cup juice from drained mandarin orange plus enough orange juice to make the measure**

2   **tablespoons grated orange rind**

¼   **teaspoon salt**

1   **cup raw rice**

1   **cup raw cashew nuts**

1   **small can mandarin orange segments**

Melt the butter and briefly sauté the celery and onion in it. Add the water, orange juice, orange rind, and salt. Bring the mixture to a boil, slowly stir in the rice, and bring to a boil again. Cover the pan, reduce the heat, and simmer about forty-five minutes or until the rice is just tender. Cook off excess moisture by removing the lid during the last few minutes if necessary. When the rice is done, stir in the cashews and orange segments.

MAKES 6 SERVINGS

PHILADELPHIA GREEN RICE

1 cup raw brown rice
2½ cups water
½ teaspoon salt
1 large onion, chopped
1 green pepper, chopped
½ cup chopped fresh parsley
1 clove garlic, minced
¼ cup salad oil
1 cup half-and-half (or milk)
1 egg, beaten
1 cup grated cheese

This recipe came from a book compiled by a group of women in Philadelphia to earn money to support a private school. If you make this, you'll either want to remain private yourself or make sure everyone likes garlic. It's utterly delicious, but the garlic is pervasive—for a long time.

Cook the rice in water, with salt added, according to the basic recipe for steamed rice. Meanwhile, chop the onion, green pepper, and parsley. Mince the garlic fine. Sauté these four ingredients briefly in the ¼ cup oil and set aside. Blend the half-and-half with the egg and mix both into the sautéed ingredients. Mix the rice and cheese together in a six-cup baking dish, pour the egg mixture over the rice and bake, covered, for one hour in a 350° F. oven.

MAKES 4–6 SERVINGS

RICE SALAD

2 cups cooked brown rice (long-grained is best here)
¼ cup chopped sweet onion
2 tablespoons pickle relish
¼ cup chopped celery
Dash salt and pepper
½ cup mayonnaise
½ teaspoon golden prepared mustard
¼ teaspoon celery seed
2 tablespoons sliced olives
2 hard-cooked eggs, sliced
Lettuce

It sounds strange, but it's good. Easy too, since you don't have to fool around paring potatoes as you do for potato salad. You'll find all the renowned gourmet cookbook writers have versions of a rice salad. After you get the basic idea you can make up your version too.

Be sure the rice is cold before you begin. Mix all the ingredients except the olives, sliced egg, and lettuce. Chill several hours. Serve surrounded with lettuce leaves and topped with the olives and sliced eggs.

MAKES 4 SERVINGS

RICE AND SHRIMP SALAD

3 to 4 cups cooked brown rice (long-grain is best here)

3 tablespoons good salad oil

½ cup chopped mild onion

½ cup chopped celery

½ cup chopped green pepper

1 cup chopped tomato

2 tablespoons chopped parsley

½ cup chopped cucumber

½ cup raw green peas (fresh or frozen)

½ cup good salad oil

2 tablespoons lemon juice

1 tablespoon cider vinegar (more or less to taste)

½ teaspoon dried dill weed

Salt and pepper

1 cup cut up, cooked, and cleaned shrimp

Lettuce

It is better to cook rice fresh for this salad than to use leftover. Be sure you've cooked out all the excess moisture. Before the rice has cooled, pour the three tablespoons oil over it and toss gently with two forks. This will keep the grains from sticking together. Cool rice, then mix in all the vegetables and the dressing. Allow the rice to stand for at least an hour in a cool place (not refrigerated), then add the shrimp. The standing period gives the dressing a chance to penetrate the rice and allows all the flavors to marry. However, the seafood should not be allowed to stand unrefrigerated. That's why you must add it last.

Serve this salad with lots of lettuce leaves, preferably one of the soft lettuces, Boston, Bibb or the like.

MAKES 4 SERVINGS

RICE WITH LENTILS

1   whole medium onion
3   tablespoons olive oil
2   cups dried lentils
½   cup rice
6   cups water
Salt
_____
1   large onion, sliced
1   tablespoon olive oil
Vinegar and yogurt

If you don't like lentils, this dish is a disaster. If you do like them, it's a dish so good you could eat it three times a day.

Brown the whole medium onion on all sides in the three table-spoons of oil in a heavy kettle. Add the lentils, rice, water, and salt. Bring to a boil over high heat, then cover the pan, lower heat, and simmer until the rice and lentils are tender, usually one or two hours. The rice will be very soft. Remove the onion from the pan and add a little water or stock if you want the mixture to be more soupy. Meanwhile, brown the large sliced onion in the olive oil. At serving time ladle the rice and lentils into big bowls, top with the fried onion and a glob of yogurt, and sprinkle with vinegar.

MAKES 6–8 SERVINGS

RICE WITH SPLIT PEAS AND SAUERKRAUT

½   cup brown rice
2   cups dried green split peas
4 to 12 cups water or stock or both
1   large onion, chopped
1   carrot, chopped
1   celery rib, chopped
1   clove garlic, minced
1   small bay leaf
1   ham bone or ham hock
1   cup sauerkraut

Don't laugh until you've tried it. This recipe grew in stages over many years. The first step began with a pot of split pea soup that turned out too watery. Penn State's football coach, Joe Paterno, said, "Put sauerkraut in it. That'll thicken it up." It sounded ghastly, but the Paternos assured me it was a good combination and, come to find out, it was. Then, as I became more interested in non-meat proteins, I learned that combining rice and legumes improved the protein quality of the resulting dish, and I began adding rice to the pea soup. Now, any other split pea soup pales in comparison.

Wash the rice if needed. Put all the ingredients except the sauer-kraut in a large soup kettle, using as much of the water or stock as you need to cover the dry ingredients by at least three inches. Bring to a boil, lower heat, cover the pan, and simmer until the peas are tender, usually about three hours, depending on the dryness of the peas. The rice will be very soft.

During the simmering period, add water or stock from time to time to maintain the consistency you prefer for soup. Some people like it so thick the spoon will stand up in it, others prefer something thin enough to drink. If there was any meat on the ham bone, pick it off, and put it back into the soup. Check the seasoning. You shouldn't need any salt because of the ham and sauerkraut. When the soup is done, stir in the sauerkraut and leave on the burner just long enough to make sure the sauerkraut has heated through. The amount of sauerkraut you use is variable. You can add lots more if you like it.

MAKES 6–8 SERVINGS

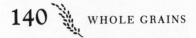

Glen Millward photo

ZUCCHINI STUFFED WITH RICE
AND CHEESE

2 **medium zucchini**
¼ **cup finely chopped onion**
1 **tablespoon butter**
¾ **cup cottage cheese**
⅔ **cup cooked brown rice**
1 **beaten egg**
2 **tablespoons chopped parsley**
Dash salt and pepper
Grated cheddar cheese

Here is a mild recipe that's nice for summer when your zucchini is overwhelming you.

Trim the ends off the zucchini and cook in a small amount of boiling water for about eight minutes, or until barely tender. Cool. Cut the zucchini in half, scoop out the centers, and chop them. Scrape away any large seeds.

Sauté the onion in the butter and then mix it with the chopped zucchini, cottage cheese, rice, egg, parsley, salt and pepper.

Fill the zucchini shells with this mixture and arrange them in a baking dish. Bake covered, for twenty-five minutes in a 350° F. oven. Remove the cover, sprinkle on the grated cheddar, and return to the oven just long enough to melt the cheese.

MAKES 4 SERVINGS

RICE WITH SWISS CHARD

1   cup chopped onion
2   cloves garlic, minced
3   tablespoons butter
2   pounds raw chard, chopped (better not to use red chard here)
4   cups cooked brown rice
4   eggs, beaten
1   cup milk plus 2 tablespoons milk powder, mixed
1½   cups grated cheddar
¼   cup chopped parsley
2   tablespoons soy sauce
Dash salt
⅛   teaspoon nutmeg
¼   cup raw sunflower seeds or any chopped raw nuts
Lemon juice or wedges

This recipe is another one for summer, when your chard is overwhelming you, and is an adaptation of a casserole in the *Moosewood Cookbook*. It sounds bland but is surprisingly tasty.

Sauté the onions and garlic in the butter until just soft. Add the chopped chard, putting in the stems first to give them a head start, and stir briefly in the butter. Lower heat a little and keep stirring and cooking for about a minute longer. Cover the pan and keep cooking until the chard is soft but not completely tender, probably only about a minute longer.

Combine the chard mixture with everything else but the seeds or nuts and lemon juice. Pack into a buttered loaf pan or baking dish and sprinkle with nuts or seeds. Bake, covered, for thirty-five minutes in a 350° F. oven.

Serve with lemon juice or wedges for each person to season his own portion.

MAKES 6 SERVINGS

RICE AND BROCCOLI CASSEROLE

¼ cup finely chopped leek (may substitute onion)

1 garlic clove, minced

1 tablespoon butter

3 cups chopped and cooked broccoli

2 cups cooked brown rice

¼ cup grated Parmesan cheese

4 eggs, beaten

½ cup milk

Salt and pepper

⅔ cup grated cheddar cheese

½ cup raw wheat germ

This makes a nice light lunch or a side dish to be served in smaller portions with an entrée. It's derived from a recipe from the people at the Rice Council of America, who ought to know, if anybody does, some good things to do with rice.

Sauté the leeks and garlic in the butter until just soft. Mix with all the remaining ingredients except the cheddar cheese and wheat germ and pour into a buttered two-quart baking dish. Sprinkle the wheat germ on top and bake until set, about thirty minutes, in a 350° F. oven. Sprinkle the cheddar cheese on top of the wheat germ and return the casserole to the oven just long enough to melt it.

MAKES 4–6 SERVINGS

BAKED RICE PUDDING

⅓ cup brown rice
4 cups whole milk
¼ to ⅓ cup honey
1 tablespoon butter
⅓ cup raisins
1 teaspoon vanilla
Cinnamon

This is the rice pudding we have eaten in my family since I was a little girl. Mother made it with white rice and used brown sugar as a sweetener; I prefer brown rice and honey. No recipe could be much easier than this one.

Wash the rice if it needs it. Mix the rice, milk, honey, and butter in a greased baking dish. Bake in a very slow oven, 225° F. to 250° F., for about six hours, stirring occasionally. The pudding is done when the rice is tender and the pudding is the thickness you like. When it reaches this point, add the raisins and vanilla, sprinkle with cinnamon, and return to the slow oven for about twenty minutes longer. Serve warm or cold.

MAKES 4 SERVINGS

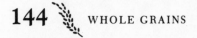

STOVE-TOP RICE PUDDING

1 cup cooked brown rice
1 cup whole milk
2 tablespoons honey
1 tablespoon butter
¼ teaspoon vanilla
2 tablespoons raisins or currants

The end result of this recipe is similar to baked rice pudding except that it takes less time to cook and you use the top of the stove instead of the oven. It's a good way to use up leftover rice.

The recipe here will make about two servings and is given in this form so you can increase it as much as you like.

Combine everything but the vanilla and raisins in a saucepan and cook over low to medium heat, depending on how much you're going to be around to stir, for about thirty minutes, more or less depending on how thick you like pudding. Interrupt cooking after twenty minutes to add vanilla and raisins.

To increase this recipe simply multiply everything by the number of cups of rice you have. Of course you'll use an equal number of cups of milk. Larger amounts may take longer to cook.

MAKES 2 SERVINGS

RICE-CUSTARD PUDDING

3 eggs
⅓ cup honey
3 cups milk
½ cup raisins
1 teaspoon vanilla
1½ cups cooked brown rice
Nutmeg

People who write cookbooks sometimes bore you to death with why they think rice pudding with eggs is better than without, or vice versa. Here's a leading contender for the with-egg type — and no further discussion of merits.

Beat together everything but the rice and nutmeg. Mix in the rice and pour into a greased two-quart baking dish. Sprinkle with the nutmeg. Set the dish in a pan of hot water and bake about 1½ hours, or until custard is set, in the 350° F. oven. Do not over-bake. The custard will continue to cook and set up some after you remove it from the oven. This is better served cold or cool, unless you are fond of the taste of hot egg custard.

MAKES 6 SERVINGS

Rice Flour

Although rice flour has no qualities to make it especially desirable to use alone, it can be substituted for wheat flour in non-yeast recipes for people who are allergic to wheat.

The Rice Council suggests substituting ¾ cup rice flour for each cup of wheat flour and increasing the leavening agents to 2½ teaspoons for each cup of rice flour you use. Below is a sample pancake recipe to illustrate this conversion.

You could adapt recipes for quick breads the same way, but I don't recommend it unless you cook for someone who is allergic to the other grains because the results tend to be crumbly and disappointing.

However, if allergy is not a problem, you can substitute small amounts of rice flour for other flours in any recipe from bread to sponge cake for variety. Recipes heavy in egg take especially well to such substitutions.

RICE FLOUR PANCAKES

1　cup rice flour
2　teaspoons baking powder
½　teaspoon baking soda
½　teaspoon salt
1¼　cups buttermilk
2　eggs, beaten
¼　cup melted butter

Sift together the dry ingredients. Combine the buttermilk, eggs, and melted butter and stir into the dry ingredients until just blended. Bake on a lightly greased hot griddle.

MAKES 2–3 SERVINGS

146

Rye

In this country people probably drink more rye than they eat, but in parts of Europe rye is still the main bread flour. Farmers often grow rye because it is the hardiest of the cereals and it will grow adequately on soils where other grains do poorly. Many use it as pasture or green manure rather than for grain. This is partly because as animal feed rye is not entirely satisfactory. It forms a sticky lump in the animal's mouth and is hard to swallow. Most farmers mix it with other grains for feeding to animals.

Although rye was originally grown mostly in the East, especially Pennsylvania, it is now grown in virtually every state in the country. Compared to other grains, rye has relatively few varieties, the most important distinction being between winter and spring varieties. Far more winter than spring rye is grown.

Winter rye is very hardy; it will survive even where temperatures go as low as − 40° F. as long as the mean winter temperature stands at about zero or higher. Rye will germinate even at temperatures in the 30s and some varieties won't germinate when the thermometer gets up around 85° F. Obviously you can grow winter rye wherever you can grow winter wheat, but also in some places where wheat wouldn't make it through the winter. You might find it a good grain for a few off-season rows in your garden, where nothing else is growing. Or plant it between rows of late vegetable crops, and you'll have a green carpet instead of a muddy lane to walk on for the final harvest.

Growing Rye

The seedbed for rye needn't be as elaborately prepared as for some grains. In the prairie states farmers often drill rye into fields still rough with the stubble of other small grains, with no further preparation. In the East and West rye is often planted in corn fields that have been disked and, sometimes, harrowed.

In garden planting, the soil should be cleaned of weeds and balanced in nutrients, although rye will tolerate a fairly poor soil. If part of your garden is more sandy than the rest, rye will do well there.

For the easiest harvesting, broadcast the seed at the rate of 1½–2 bushels per acre (that's about three pounds for 1,000 square feet) in broad rows, leaving space between them for cultivation. That should produce about thirty bushels per acre, or forty to forty-five pounds per 1,000 square feet. (And remember, that seed you're planting is rye, *not* rye grass.) Winter rye should be planted in late summer or early fall. Many recommend planting about the time of the first frost. That way the rye will grow four to six inches high. Farmers often use it then for late fall pasturage, without diminishing the harvest the next year. Rye is planted a little later than winter wheat.

Spring rye can be planted as early as the ground can be worked since, unlike corn, rye will germinate in cold soil. Whichever time planting is done in your area, you will have little

ERGOT

We've purposely avoided long dissertations on grain diseases in this book. Your chances for avoiding them are excellent if you raise only small plots of grain.

But ergot — that's different. You should be able to identify and avoid eating rye that has been infected with it.

Ergot is a disease of rye caused by a fungus that infects the plants when they are in blossom. You'll know your rye has this disease if, when you see the grains developing, you notice small, black, grain-size growths replacing the individual grains. These are called sclerotia. They are poisonous, both to us and our livestock.

You may never spot ergot in the rye you grow. If you do, we recommend destroying that grain.

Martin and Leonard, in Principles of Field Crop Production, suggest harvesting the rye, then immersing it in a 20 percent solution of common salt, and stirring the grain, so that the ergot bodies will float to the surface and can be skimmed off. The rye then should be washed and dried, to remove the salt.

to do afterwards except keep down the worst of the weeds until harvest time.

Harvesting

You harvest and store rye exactly as you would wheat, so see the chapter on wheat for instructions. Rye ripens earlier than wheat, and ripeness can be tested the same way you test wheat for ripeness.

Rye does not have a hull, so it is ready for cooking or grinding when harvested, and is easier to grind than some of the other grains.

Rye straw is prized for many uses. It is tall — five or six feet — and has a beautiful golden color. It is the favorite straw around horse stalls. You can also experiment with it in several crafts.

In Germany rye used to be sown much thicker than usual if it was to be used in crafts. This kept the blades from growing too fast. It was harvested when it was about eighteen inches high, by tearing the stalks out by the roots, tying them into small bundles, and letting them dry a day or so in the sun. Then the bundles were hung up under cover to season for a year or two. Before using the straw, craftspeople had to open the bundles and spread them out to expose the straw to two nights of dew and three days of sun on each side, bleaching and softening the stalks. Finally, the heads and roots were cut from the stalks and the stalks were sorted into piles according to thickness to be worked into baskets, hats, mats, and even such large items as trunks.

All this sounds like a lot of work and certainly we have no contemporary guides to such a process, but if you wanted to experiment with rye straw for fun rather than for food or profit, you probably could produce some unique craft items and become a modern-day pioneer in straw craft.

Buying Rye

If you're not interested in straw or green manure and you just want to try a few recipes, you may decide to buy your rye. It is sold in whole berry form in natural-food stores; a few places may also carry it cracked, but this is less common. Most natural-food stores now stock rolled rye or rye flakes, which look much like oat or wheat flakes and are used the same way. You can also find rye flour and rye meal at food stores. The meal is only a coarser grind of flour and works as well as finer flours in baking bread.

Letting the wind do the work.

149

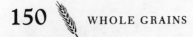

You will notice some rye flours are darker than others and may be labeled "light," "medium," or "dark," depending on how much bran has been sifted out in processing, and the variety of rye from which the flour was milled. But in spite of looking a little different, all rye flours taste about the same and are fairly interchangeable in bread recipes.

A good reason for buying flour rather than grinding your own is that the whole rye berries are comparatively soft, and so tend to clog a stone grinder. They can be ground in mills that have steel blades.

Using Rye

Almost everybody likes the taste of rye in one form or another, although the authors of one cookbook said they deliberately omitted any recipes using whole rye berries because they take "hours to cook" and taste "just dreadful." Wrong on both counts. The only reason rye berries might taste dreadful is that they were cooked so long they got gooey. You've probably seen more than one recipe instructing you to cook a whole grain for as long as three hours, but the fact is, rye berries shouldn't be cooked much more than thirty minutes if you want them to retain their shape and texture. If you want to make a porridge or gruel of rye, you'd do it just as you make oatmeal, simply cooking the whole, cracked, or rolled grain and water together until it's very tender and mushy, but that seems to be wasting the potential of a grain that can be cooked in many more exotic and delicious ways.

Many of the recipes in this section begin with *cooked* rye berries, so even though you'll probably not serve just plain cooked rye very often, we'll begin with that basic recipe.

COOKED RYE BERRIES

2 cups whole rye berries
4 cups water

Wash the rye before cooking by running water over it in the pan and tilting the pan to run off the floating chaff and dust. Do this step carefully, for rye can taste dirty if it hasn't been cleaned well.

Cover the rye berries with the water and bring quickly to a boil over high heat. Reduce heat, cover the pan, and simmer about thirty minutes, or just until a few of the grains have begun to burst open. Drain the grain in a colander or sieve; all the moisture probably will *not* have been absorbed.

MAKES ABOUT 4 CUPS COOKED RYE

VEGETABLE-RYE CASSEROLE

4 cups pieces of carrot, cauliflower, and broccoli, mixed (fresh or frozen)
½ cup water
1 leek
1 large celery stalk
¼ cup chopped parsley
2 tablespoons butter
2 cups cooked rye berries

¼ cup butter
¼ cup unbleached white flour
2 cups stock
¼ cup dry white wine
½ teaspoon salt
½ teaspoon white pepper

¼ to ½ cup wheat germ or dry bread crumbs

Cook the carrots, cauliflower, and broccoli together in the ½ cup water until the vegetables are barely tender. Set them aside, using any remaining cooking water to make up part of the two cups stock.

Chop the leek and celery fine and sauté, along with the parsley, in the two tablespoons butter. You may substitute onion for the leek, but use the leek if you possibly can because its sweetness complements the taste of the rye in a way no onion can.

In a two-quart baking dish, combine the steamed and sautéed vegetables with the cooked rye. Mix together well and set aside while you make the sauce.

Melt the ¼ cup butter in a sauce pan, stir in the flour, and stir over medium heat until the roux is golden. Gradually whisk in the stock, cooking and stirring to make a light sauce. When it is smooth and hot, season with the dry white wine and the salt and pepper. Cook a few minutes longer to evaporate the alcohol from the wine.

Pour the sauce over the vegetables in the baking dish, using a spoon to make sure the sauce gets well mixed in. Sprinkle enough wheat germ or bread crumbs over the top of the vegetables to cover the surface and bake in a 350° F. oven for thirty to forty-five minutes, or until the top is browned and the contents of the dish are bubbling.

MAKES 8 SERVINGS

FRIED RYE

2 tablespoons butter
2 tablespoons chopped parsley
2 tablespoons chopped leek or shallot
½ cup chopped raw mushrooms
2 tablespoons chopped celery
2 cups cooked rye berries
½ teaspoon salt

The Chinese should eat their hearts out if they don't have this recipe. It's like fried rice, only better. Rye prepared this way is absolutely delicious, especially if you serve it with pork chops and brown gravy.

Melt the butter in a large skillet, preferably iron. Keep the heat as high as you can without burning the butter and rapidly stir in the parsley, leek, mushrooms, and celery. Stir and cook until the leek is just beginning to brown. The celery should still be crisp. Stir in the rye berries that have been cooked and drained (leftover is fine), add salt, and stir over medium high heat until all the grains are coated with butter and are just beginning to brown.

MAKES 6–8 SERVINGS

RYE AND PARSNIPS

3 cups peeled and diced parsnips
1 cup water
2 cups cooked rye berries

¼ cup butter
¼ cup unbleached white flour
2 cups milk and parsnip cooking water
½ cup grated sharp cheddar cheese
½ teaspoon salt
Chopped chives

This combination is so good you could serve it at the most important dinner party you ever give—provided you're not entertaining someone who doesn't like parsnips. Even then it might be worth the risk; few tastes complement each other as perfectly as those of rye and parsnips.

Cook the parsnips in the water until they are tender but not mushy. Cut out any pieces of core that are too woody to cook well. Mix the cooked parsnips and rye berries and set aside where you can keep them warm.

Make a medium-to-thin sauce by melting the butter, stirring in the unbleached white flour, and cooking to golden. Whisk in the milk and parsnip cooking liquid (for a total of two cups liquid). Cook and stir over medium heat until hot and smooth, then stir in all but two tablespoons of the cheese and the salt. Stir until the cheese melts. If the sauce seems thick, thin it out with a little more milk because for this recipe the sauce should not be too thick.

To serve, pour the hot sauce over the warm rye and parsnips and sprinkle with the remaining cheese and chopped chives. Serve very hot.

MAKES 8 SERVINGS

Fried rye berries.

Glen Millward photo

MARINATED VEGETABLE AND RYE SALAD

Baby limas
Corn
Green beans in 1-inch
   pieces
Pearl onions
Sliced carrots
Brussels sprouts

Cooked rye berries
Sliced raw radish
Cooked chick peas
Diced raw cucumber

This was inspired by a salad served at the Millheim Hotel in Pennsylvania, but the only thing the two recipes have in common is that they both contain rye berries. Experiments in cooking often work that way; you taste something good, pick out one thing you like about it, and run off on a series of related-but-not-very experiments. In any case, the rye grains in something called "Perfect Protein Salad" triggered the experiments that led to this marinated vegetable salad.

In a large glass bowl or jar make layers of the vegetables in the first group, cooked just to the crisp stage and cooled.

Next add layers of rye berries, radish, chick peas, and raw cucumber.

Over the entire mixture, pour a marinade of ¼ cup wine vinegar for each cup salad oil (part olive is nice), which you have seasoned with dill weed, garlic, and salt and pepper. To get the right garlic flavor, soak a peeled garlic clove in the oil for an hour or two, then discard the clove.

Refrigerate until everything is thoroughly chilled. Serve in the glass container so that the layers show. At the Millheim Hotel, the cook studied this recipe and said, "I'll have to make two—one for people to look at and one for them to eat."

RYE BORSCHT

1 small head cabbage
1 large onion
2 stalks celery
3 cloves fresh garlic, peeled and minced
½ bay leaf
4 cups canned or cooked tomatoes
2 cups canned or cooked beets, diced
Water or stock
2 cups cooked rye berries
1 cup cooked white beans
3 tablespoons cider vinegar
3 tablespoons brown sugar
Salt and pepper
Yogurt or sour cream

If you use vegetable stock rather than beef or chicken stock, this is a fine vegetarian soup-stew. Either way, it's a satisfying meal. One taster pronounced it "so good it hurts."

Chop all the raw vegetables coarsely and put them into a good-sized soup kettle with the garlic, bay leaf, tomatoes, and beets. Add water or stock to cover and simmer gently with the lid on until all the vegetables are tender. Add the cooked rye and white beans and simmer a few minutes more over very low heat to allow the flavors to marry. During this simmering time, season with the vinegar, brown sugar, and salt and pepper. This should have a decided sweet-sour taste, so add a little more vinegar and brown sugar, in equal amounts, if it isn't pronounced enough.

Serve topped with lots of yogurt or sour cream.

And no matter how skeptical you feel about the garlic, don't use less or omit it or substitute garlic powder because the flavor of fresh, long-cooked garlic is mild and delicious and an essential part of the flavors in borscht.

MAKES 12 GENEROUS SERVINGS

RYE PANCAKES

1¼ cups rye flour
1 teaspoon baking soda
½ teaspoon salt
2 eggs
2 cups buttermilk
2 tablespoons melted
   butter
1 tablespoon honey

You can make pancakes out of practically anything. These of rye are delicate and unusual.

Sift together the dry ingredients. Separate the eggs, beat the yolks into the buttermilk, and whip the whites until they are stiff but not dry. Stir the butter and honey into the buttermilk-egg mixture, and then stir the liquids into the dry mixture, mixing well but without hard beating. Finally, fold the whipped egg whites into the batter thoroughly but gently. Mix a little more than you would for a soufflé, but try not to knock too much of the air out of the whites, because they're part of the leavening.

Pour onto a lightly greased hot griddle, about ¼ cupful at a time, and bake until the bubbles show on the uncooked side. Turn and bake until the bubble side is golden brown. Serve at once. Instead of a heavy syrup like molasses or maple with these delicate pancakes, try something with a little zing—raspberry jelly, thinned to syrup with a bit of water, perhaps.

MAKES 3–4 SERVINGS

RYE BREAD STICKS

1 package active dry
   yeast
1¼ cup warm water
   (90°–105°)
1 teaspoon sugar
2 cups unbleached
   white flour
1 cup rye flour
1½ cups more unbleached
   white flour
1 egg beaten with
1 tablespoon cold water
Caraway seeds

Dissolve the yeast in the warm water and stir in the sugar. Allow the mixture to stand until it is bubbling, then mix in the two cups unbleached flour and beat vigorously until the batter is smooth and elastic and pulls away from the sides of the bowl in long strings. Beat in the rye flour and mix very well. Finally, work in as much more white flour as you need to make a dough you can handle. Knead until it is smooth and stretchy. Place in a greased bowl in a warm place and allow to double in bulk. Punch down and allow to rest about five minutes, then break off pieces of dough and shape them into rope-like sticks as long as you want the finished sticks to be, but only about half as thick. Arrange the sticks on greased baking sheets, allowing space between for them to rise without touching each other.

Let stand until the sticks have risen to about double, then brush with a mixture of the beaten egg and tablespoon cold water and sprinkle with caraway seeds. Bake in a 475° F. oven about ten minutes, or until the sticks are brown. Increase or reduce baking time as needed for the size sticks you shaped.

Rye Breads

You could make rye bread according to a different recipe every day of the week for a year without repeating yourself. However, as you ate your way through all that bread, you'd find all the recipes fell into three basic groups: rye breads using wheat in the dough, all-rye or mostly-rye breads, and sourdough ryes. The rye breads that include a goodly amount of wheat are usually springy to the bite and sweet. All-rye and mostly-rye breads are dense, heavy, and don't rise high because of the low gluten content of the flour. Sourdough ryes can be sweet, but usually are less so than regular yeast ryes, and they usually contain at least *some* wheat flour. We'll include one example from each group here, so that as you encounter other rye bread recipes you'll be able to tell by studying the ingredients what kind of bread each recipe will produce.

MOSTLY RYE BREAD

1   package active dry yeast
¼   cup warm water (90°–105° F.)
2   cups potato cooking water
1   tablespoon honey
2   teaspoons salt
1   tablespoon oil
2   cups unbleached white flour
1   cup mashed or riced potatoes
4   cups rye flour

Dissolve the yeast in the warm water and add it to the potato water, which should be warm but not hot. Add the honey, salt, and oil. Gradually beat in the white flour, being sure to continue beating until the mixture gets shiny. Beat in the mashed potatoes and, a little at a time, the rye flour. Continue beating in flour until you have a dough you can handle, then dump it onto a floured surface, shape it into a ball, cover with a cloth, and allow it to rest fifteen minutes before beginning to knead. Kneading this dough will be easier if you grease your hands first and keep extra flour available to work in as the dough gets sticky. Knead for ten to twenty minutes — this dough will never get as stretchy and shiny as an all-wheat dough because there's less gluten in the mixture.

Put the kneaded dough in a warm place to rise until doubled in bulk; punch it down; shape it into two loaves for 9 × 5-inch (or smaller) greased pans. One-pound coffee cans work, too.

Let the loaves rise again, in the pans, until about double. Bake in a preheated 375° F. oven for about sixty minutes.

MAKES 2 SMALL LOAVES

SOURDOUGH RYE

1 cup sourdough starter
1 cup unbleached white flour
1 cup rye flour
1 cup water

2 cups rye flour
2 cups boiling water
½ cup honey
⅓ cup butter
2 teaspoons salt
About 5 cups (total) rye and unbleached white flour mixed half and half
Cornmeal

You can be overwhelmed by the number of different recipes for sourdough rye. Some of them are quite complicated and must be started as much as four days ahead of baking time; some involve making two or even three sponges. I still remember trying one such multi-step recipe back in the days when I was new to the kitchen. The recipe required making two sponges and keeping everything warm and growing over a period of three days, which involved putting the mixing bowl under the furnace housing and checking on it every few hours. The finished loaves were supposed to be crusty. Crusty turned out to be an understatement. Ultimately, after having chipped a bread knife and bent a carving knife, we had to get a hacksaw out of the toolbox to cut the bread. A neighbor said it was quite good, ". . . once you got in."

This recipe is much simpler and should produce loaves you can cut with an ordinary bread knife.

Mix the first four ingredients in a large bowl the day before you want to bake the bread. Cover the bowl loosely and allow to stand in a warm place to ferment for at least eight hours—longer is better.

At baking time, combine the rye flour, boiling water, honey, butter, and salt, mix well, and allow to cool. When you are sure the mix-

ture is cool enough not to kill the yeast in the starter (below 105° F.), combine the two mixtures, beating well. Then stir in as much of the rye/wheat flour combination as you need to make a dough you can handle. Turn it onto a floured surface, shape into a ball, and allow it to stand, covered with a damp cloth, for fifteen minutes before kneading. Knead until the dough is shiny and springy. Place it in a large greased bowl to double in bulk. When it has doubled, punch it down and allow it to rise again. Shape into three round loaves and place them on a cookie sheet which has been sprinkled heavily with cornmeal. Allow the loaves to rise until doubled in bulk. Bake in a preheated 350° F. oven for fifty to sixty minutes. If you like a heavy crust and have a good hacksaw, brush the loaves with cold water several times during the baking period.

MAKES 3 ROUND LOAVES

SWEET RYE BREAD WITH WHEAT

1 package active dry yeast

½ cup warm water (90°–105° F.)

1 teaspoon sugar

2 cups boiling water

2 cups dark rye flour

¾ cup blackstrap molasses

⅓ cup butter

2 teaspoons salt

6 to 7 cups unbleached white flour

Cornmeal

Dissolve the yeast in the warm water, along with the sugar. Allow to stand until frothy. Meanwhile, pour the boiling water over the rye flour, add the molasses, butter, and salt, and let the mixture stand until it is cooled to lukewarm. Be sure to let it cool long enough because if it's too hot, you'll kill the yeast, the bread won't rise, and you'll end up baking rye bricks. After the yeast begins to froth, stir in several spoonsful of the white flour to give the yeast something to feed on while the rye mixture cools. This is kind of a mock-sourdough procedure and won't affect the taste of the bread.

When you are sure the rye mixture is cool enough, beat in the yeast and two cups of the white flour. Beat this very hard with a wooden spoon, until you've worked up the gluten and the dough becomes shiny and elastic. Then gradually beat in more and more of the flour until you have a dough you can handle. Cover it with a cloth and allow it to stand for fifteen minutes before kneading. Then knead, using additional white flour if needed, until the dough is elastic. You'll never completely eliminate stickiness when you knead a rye bread, so at some point, after about ten minutes of kneading, you just have to declare yourself "done" and put the dough into a greased bowl to rise in a warm place.

When the dough has doubled in bulk, punch it down, cover the bowl with a damp cloth, and allow to rise again until nearly doubled. Punch down again and divide the dough into three equal parts. Cover them and let them rest while you prepare a large cookie sheet by sprinkling it with cornmeal. Shape the dough into three round loaves with all the creases and seams on the bottom. Allow the loaves to rise on the cookie sheet until they have doubled in bulk. Bake in a preheated 350° F. oven for fifty to sixty minutes, or until the loaves sound hollow when you turn them upside down and thump the bottoms.

MAKES 3 SMALL LOAVES

PEASANT BLACK BREAD

1 cup water
1 cup coffee
½ cup cornmeal
1 tablespoon butter
2 teaspoons salt
2 tablespoons molasses
1 tablespoon unsweet-
    ened cocoa powder
1 package active dry
    yeast
1 tablespoon sugar
1 tablespoon flour
¼ cup warm water
    (90°–105° F.)
2 cups rye flour, pre-
    ferably dark
1 cup whole wheat flour
Unbleached white flour

Almost everybody who has a sourdough rye recipe also tries a black bread. Although much of the flour is rye, you'll see that this recipe defies the categories into which the rye breads usually fall. It's nearly a pumpernickle because it contains some cornmeal, but pumpernickle usually contains mashed potatoes and this recipe doesn't use them. Not only that, the bread isn't really black. Bakers have tried all kinds of ingredients to make bread "black"—coffee, chocolate, Postum, caramel color, even grape juice. But if the coloring ingredients taste strongly in the finished product, you still don't have good black bread. Maybe we're pursuing a fairy tale item that exists more convincingly in our minds than in reality. Anyhow, for the record, here's a "black" bread recipe in which you can't taste the coloring ingredients. It's adapted from one used by James Beard.

Bring the coffee and water to a boil in a small pan and sprinkle in the cornmeal, stirring rapidly with a whisk to avoid lumps. Remove from the heat as soon as the mixture is thick and stir in the butter, salt, molasses, and cocoa. Set this mixture aside to cool. Combine the yeast, sugar, tablespoon flour, and warm water in a small bowl and set it aside to "grow."

When the cornmeal mixture is lukewarm and you're sure it is no longer hot enough to kill the yeast, combine the two mixtures in a large bowl. Begin working in the flours, beginning with the rye, then the whole wheat, and finally, as much unbleached white flour as you need for making a dough you can handle, and for kneading. If the mixture seems to be getting too stiff and dry before you have all the rye and whole wheat flours worked in, add water, a little at a time. It mixes in quite easily. The quantities specified for liquids here are necessarily vague because so much depends on the moisture content of the flours and on how long you cook the cornmeal.

When you have a dough you can handle, knead vigorously. It will never completely lose its stickiness, but will become springy and pleasant to handle. Allow to rise in a large, greased bowl in a warm place until doubled in bulk, then shape into two round balls and place them in greased eight-inch pie tins or in small round greased metal bowls. Allow to rise to double, and bake in a preheated 375° F. oven for fifty to sixty minutes. Brush the top of the loaves with cold water before baking and, if you want the crust hard, several times during baking as well.

MAKES 2 SMALL LOAVES

Appendix

Whole Grains

If you decide to buy instead of growing grain, and can't find what you want in your local supermarket or natural-food store, try one of these:

Arrowhead Mills, Inc.
Box 866
Hereford TX 79045

CC Grains
6749 East Marginal
    Way South
Seattle WA 98108

Deer Valley Farm
RD 1
Guilford NY 13780

The Grover Co.
2111 S. Industrial
    Park Ave.
Tempe AZ 85282

Sunburst Farms
20 South Kellogg
Goleta CA 93117

Walnut Acres
Penns Creek PA 17862

Chico-San Inc.
Chico CA 95926
(rice and rice products)

Hand Grain Grinders

These hand-powered gristmills will meet your demand if it is only for a few cups of flour.

BH Grain Mill
Agri Resources
RR3, Napanee
Ontario K7R 3K8
Canada

Corona
R&R Mill Co.
45 West First North
Smithfield, UT 84335

Quaker City
Nelson's and Sons
PO Box 1296
Salt Lake City, UT
    84110

The more ambitious user of grains will want a powered mill. Here are a few of the many companies manufacturing them:

Marathon Flour Mill
The Grover Co.
2111 S. Industrial Park
    Ave.
Tempe, AZ 85282

Mil-Rite Flour Mill
Retsel Corp.
Box 47
McCammon, ID 83250

Excalibur Flour Mill
Excalibur Products
57711 Florin-Perkins
Rd.
Sacramento, CA 95828

Magic Mill II
Magic Mill
235 West 200 South
Salt Lake City, UT
84101

Magic Mill II.

Harvesting Tools

The would-be grain grower is discouraged most often, not by the difficulties of growing grains, for they are few, or the grinding and use of them, but by those steps in between. Grain must be harvested, detached from its straw, separated from its chaff, often separated too from its hull.

With most grains these steps are not impossible for the grower of a small amount of grain. But they are slow for the person who wishes to

grow enough grain for his animals, or perhaps for sale or barter.

In these United States there's a long step between the sickle-it-and-beat-it-and-blow-it method and use of that giant charger of the Wheat Belt, the combine, that will cut, thresh, winnow, and clean the grain crop, then either bag the grain or spew it into a truck or trailer.

But what of the homesteader or home-grain-grower whose tiny patch might be swallowed up and spewed forth by this behemoth in one bite? There's little on the market for him except for antiques, some still serviceable, lying forgotten in barns on farms where once they earned their keep and more.

This is not so in Europe and Asia. Both of these continents still have farmers raising grain for their own use, much as it was done a century ago in this country. And they have tools and equipment to handle crops this size efficiently and inexpensively.

Here are some companies that provide information on their products:

CeCoCo
Box 8, Ibaraki City
Osaka Pref. 567
Japan

This company's catalog displays an array of equipment for the small farmer, including a reaper-binder, power and foot-operated thresher and several small combines.

Central States Mainline Distributors
Box 348
London, OH 43140

Distributes the BCS binder, a unit that mounts on a walking tractor and cuts and ties bundles of grain.

Iseki Agricultural Machinery Co.
1-3, Nihonbashi 2-chrome, Chuo-ku
Tokyo 103, Japan

Manufactures a variety of small equipment, including a reaper-binder and two models of small combines.

Kincaid Equipment Manufacturing Corp.
Box 471
Haven, KS 67543

Manufactures several models of the K.E.M. combines.

Poynter Products, Ltd.
52 Greenaway St.
Bulleen, Victoria, Australia

Manufactures a small stripper-harvester unit that plucks the grain heads, then threshes and winnows the grain.

Scythe and Cradle

The scythe is easy to find in hardware stores, farm catalogs, and at auctions. But the cradle? Look in a museum, you say. We said it also, until recently. Now we have found a source. For information on this, and other tools for haying and for harvesting grains, write to:

By Hand & Foot Ltd.
Box 611
Brattleboro, VT 05301

Grain Cleaners

The tried-and-true method of cleaning grain by pouring it from container to container on a breezy day works fine for relatively small amounts. For larger amounts, or for those who want very clean grain, here are some manufacturers or distributors of grain cleaners:

Sears
Farm and Ranch Catalog

A Sears unit was used in the Garden Way tests. Does a fine job.

Burrows Equipment Co.
1316 Sherman Ave.
Evanston IL 60204

Units of various capacities.

Seedburo Equipment Co.
1022 W. Jackson Blvd.
Chicago, IL 60606

Among its offerings is a hand-operated barley pearler.

Rice Hullers

CeCoCo in Japan (see address under Harvesting Tools) has several rice hullers and polishers. A huller produces brown rice; use of a polisher converts the rice to white rice, removing the hull, bran and germ—and most of the nutrition of this grain.

Power rice hullers and polishers are sold by:

Engleberg Huller Co.
Box 277
Factoryville, PA 18419

Index

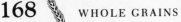

Other Garden Way Books You Will Enjoy

The home gardener and cook concerned about healthful eating will find an up-to-date library essential. Here are some excellent books from the publisher of *Whole Grains*.

Revised KEEPING THE HARVEST: Home Storage of Fruits & Vegetables

Most up-to-date information available on canning, freezing, bottling, pickling, steam juicing, curing, drying and more. Plus how to build and use root cellars and storage containers (indoors and out)! Loaded with helpful hints, photos, and recipes.
244 pp.   Order #45 $7.95

SAUCE IT! Making Sauces, Purees and Gravies from Fruits & Vegetables

Take your blender, food mill, Squeezo Strainer, or food processor and simply make a quick puree of tomatoes, apples any fresh vegetable or fruit. Then use them fresh in over 170 recipes or learn the best ways to preserve them for future use. A one-of-a-kind guide to *home food preservation*.
172 pp.   Order #109 $5.95

Sweet & Hard CIDER

Unique, attractive and incredibly complete! How to make, use and enjoy sweet cider, sparkling and champagne ciders, applejack, brandy, cider vinegar and more! Plus color photos to aid in apple identification; even how to deal with cider and the law.
272 pp.   Order #54 $9.95

MAKING HOMEMADE SOUPS & STEWS

Hearty Stews. Chowders. Gumbos, chilies and soups — hot and cold, clear and creamy.
184 pp.   Order #102 $4.95

THE GARDEN WAY BREAD BOOK

Over 140 all-natural, all-delicious recipes guaranteed to please both novice and experienced bakers alike. Plus, ideas for fitting bread-making around a busy schedule and "can't-fail" instructions for simple, fragrant loaves.
192 pp.   Order #95 $8.95

THE SPROUTER'S COOKBOOK: For Fast Kitchen Crops

Easy-to-grow, high-protein, fresh greens year 'round. Specifics in 11 varieties. Plus 135 delicious recipes — soups to desserts.
144 pp   Order #13 $4.95

Garden Way's GUIDE TO FOOD DRYING: How to Dehydrate, Store and Use Vegetables, Fruits and Herbs

The practical, low-cost alternative to canning and freezing. How to do it, what equipment to use, how to make your own dehydrator, plus hundreds of delicious, nutritious recipes for using what you've dried.
242 pp.   Order #21 $5.95

THE SOYBEAN BOOK: Growing and Using Nature's Miracle Protein

Over 200 recipes — everything from soups to casseroles to desserts. Information on growing, harvesting and storing soybeans.
172 pp.   Order #75 $5.95

WOODSTOVE COOKERY

Complete guide to cooking the "old fashioned" way with 201 delicious recipes, whether you have a wood cookstove or not! Information on buying and installing a wood cookstove, cleaning and operating, too.
106 pp.   Order #107 $5.95

These Garden Way books are available at your bookstore or may be ordered directly from Garden Way Publishing, Dept. 171X, Charlotte, Vermont 05445. If your order is less than $10, please add 75¢ postage and handling.